ORASAIGH

Steve Ely's previous publications include a novel, *Ratmen*, a biography, *Ted Hughes's South Yorkshire*, and a dozen books or pamphlets of poetry, including *Oswald's Book of Hours*, *Englaland*, *Lectio Violant*, *The European Eel*, *Lives of British Shrews*, and *Eely*. He's been visiting South Uist for fifteen years or so and the landscape around the little tidal island of Orasaigh has become his favourite place on the planet.

Michael Faint is a photographer who lives on the Isle of South Uist. Recent solo exhibitions include *Innse Gall* and *Cladach | Shore*. Shortlisted for the Sony World Photography Awards, his work is published and exhibited widely.

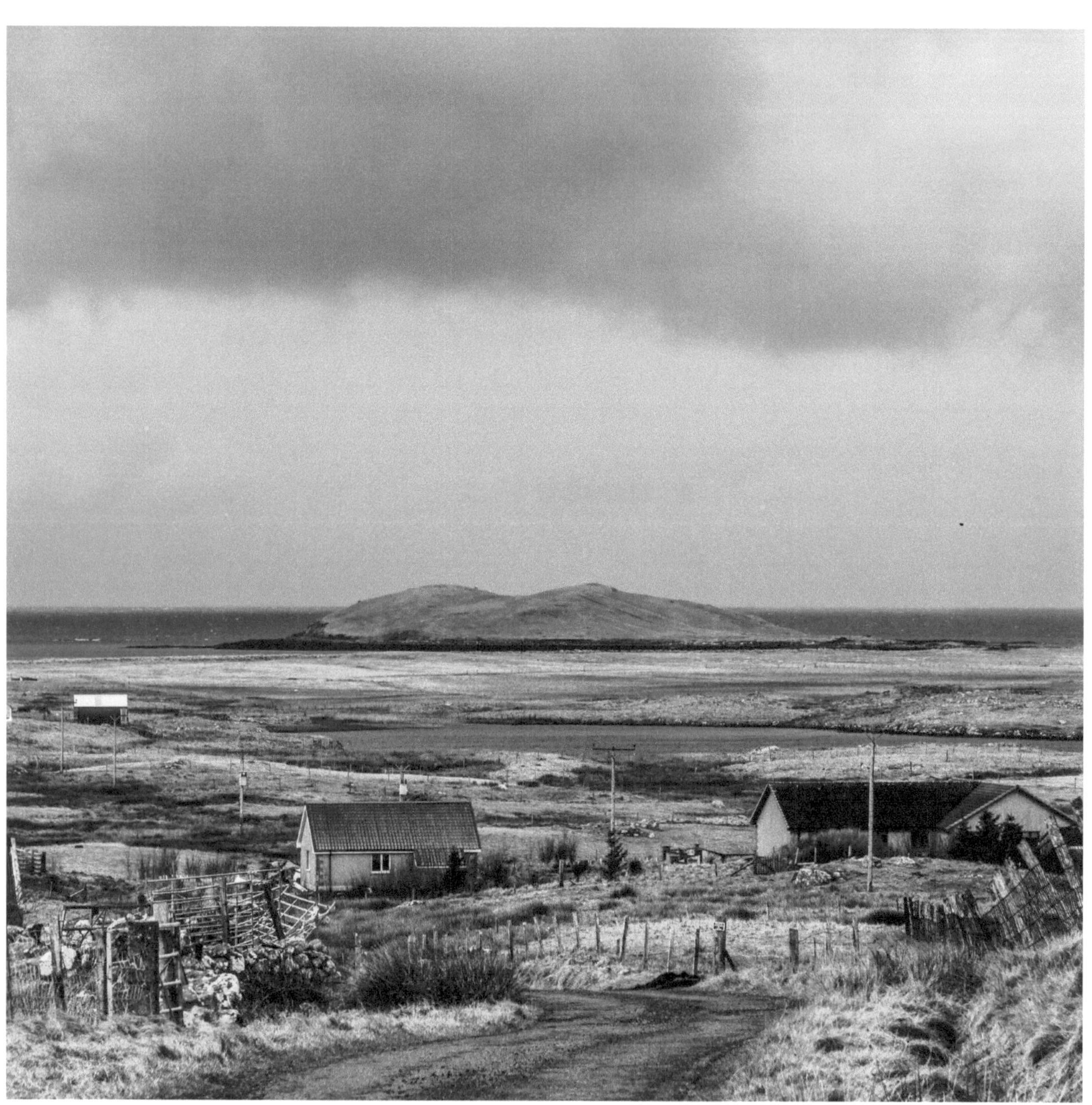

CONTENTS

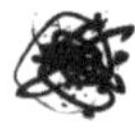

ISBN: 978-1-916938-93-9

Cover designed by Aaron Kent

Edited and Typeset by Aaron Kent

Broken Sleep Books Ltd
PO BOX 102
Llandysul
SA44 9BG

Orasaigh

Steve Ely
&
Michael Faint

Broken Sleep Books

The poem is for Uist.
The photographs are for Sarah.

ORASAIGH

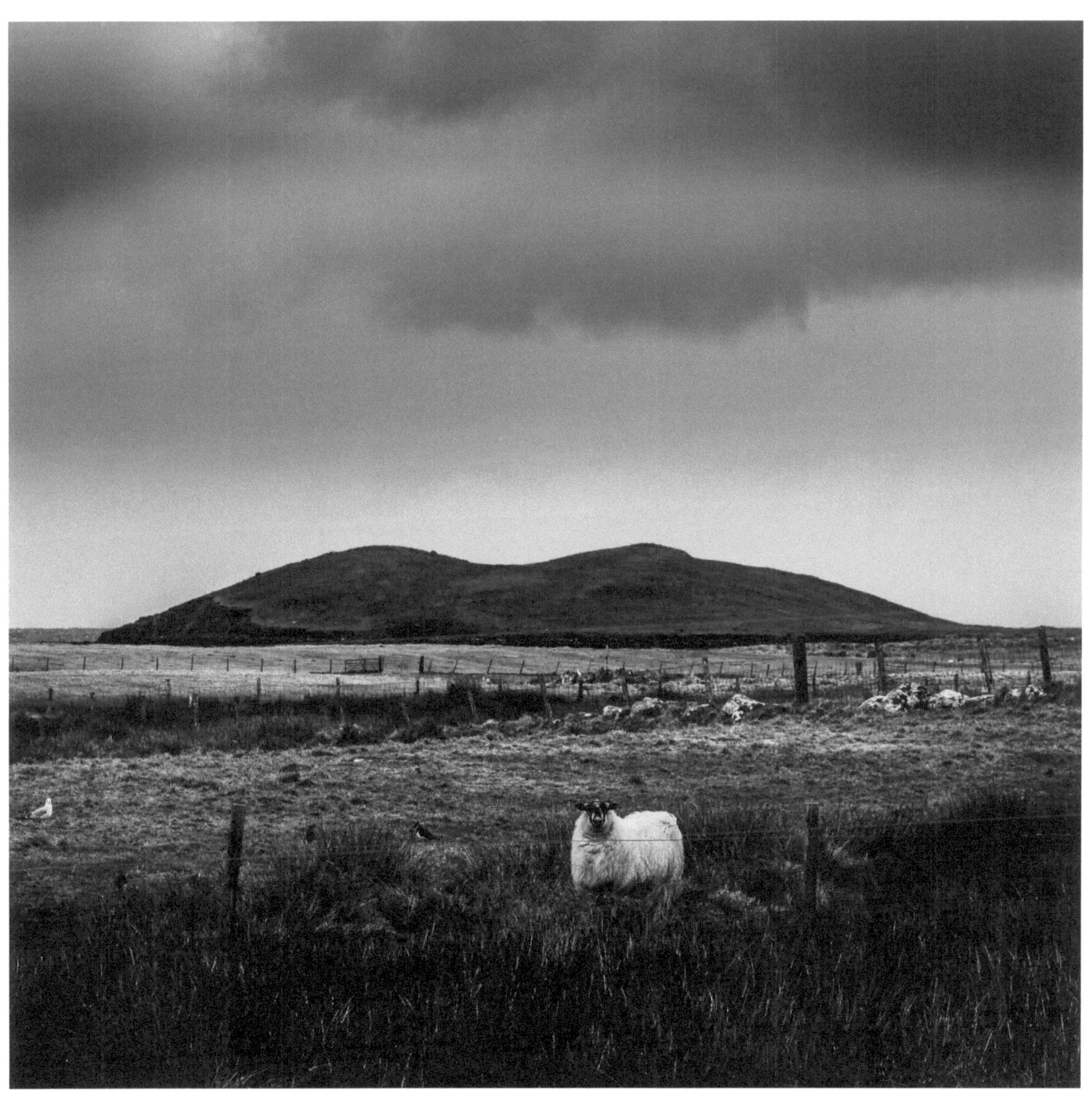

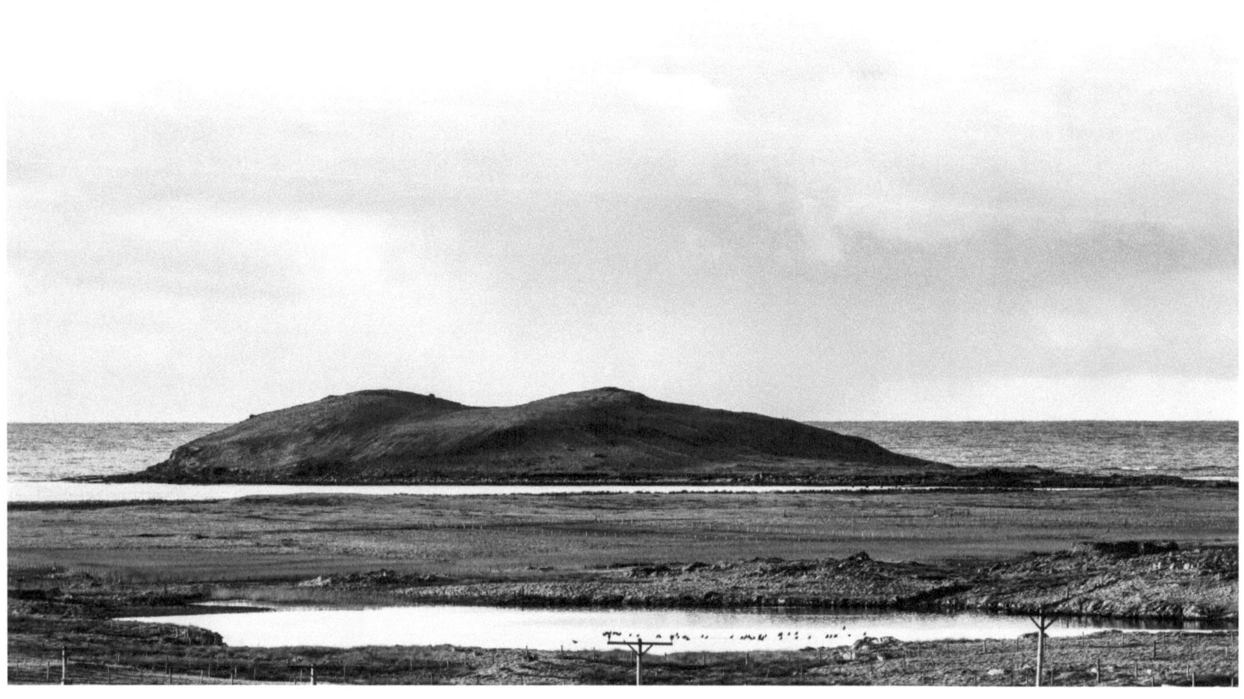

I

From the midsummer height of Càireasbhal,
looking west over causewayed Dùn na Cille,
the sun has lit the townlands in the Gulf Stream's evening zephyr.
In the pellucid ocean light, under the troposphere's
argentine blue, everything comes into HD focus:
the blackland's dikes and rickety fences,
rush-fledged forage of tussock and rock,
fleece-shedding sheep and rough, red-pelted shorthorns;
Boisdale's straggle of crofts and cottages,
Nissen huts, tractors, jacked-up transits;
and the tracks beyond through the plain of barley,
to the sugar-sand crescent of Orasaigh Bagh.
Orasaigh, the double-humped tidal island
on the beach off the edge of the Boisdale machair,
still moored to her mother by the sand umbilicus
she fashions herself from the silts of the longshore drift.
She rises on her strand like a sagging frame tent,
Or the sunken withers of a sea-ware pony,
two shaggy rorquals, breaking the swell
from the Sound of Barra, frozen on the curve
towards Hirte and the Greenland seas.
The beach-stripping blitzkrieg of winter storms
and the rising tides of the gnawing Atlantic
have frayed, but not in centuries severed,
her squat tombolo's hawser. She will not let go
of the land that birthed her and to which she still belongs.

II

I walk the track from Leth Meadhanach
to the crossroads with the faded road
that runs from Pol a' Charra to the Ford.
A quarter-mile strip of rough and tumble grazing:
horsetails, juncus, clumps of yellow flag,
rocks breaching the turf like the hulks
of fossilised right whales. The isle lies flat
on the low horizon, crushed under the dome
of the huge Atlantic sky. Each crunching stride-length
lifts it taller, on the western skyline, the vistas
of my mind. I lift the loop on the five-bar gate
and pass between derelict lazybeds and a stand
of thin phragmites. Sheep scatter from the fences
at my bootscrapes. Greylags up their periscopes.
Redshank yammer from the trackside posts
and switchback lapwings puit and dive—a motorhome
rumbles down the track to the barbecue pits
and picnic tables of the Geàrraidh na Mònadh campsite.
Settling dust, crushed stone diminuendo:
corncrakes shorting from the eight-inch grass
under tremolo columns of larks;
ululating snipe traverse the argentinian blue.
The crossroads mark the blackland's end
and the start of a furlong of sandy machair,
the ever-unravelling remnant of the miles-wide
Bronze Age plain. I set a course across the headlands,
between rusty ploughs and abandoned rollers,
sunk axle-deep in the blown sand's sod.
The patchwork of barley and needlework fallow
lays down its quilt before me, washed green silks
with crimson crewellings, stitched with cobalt,

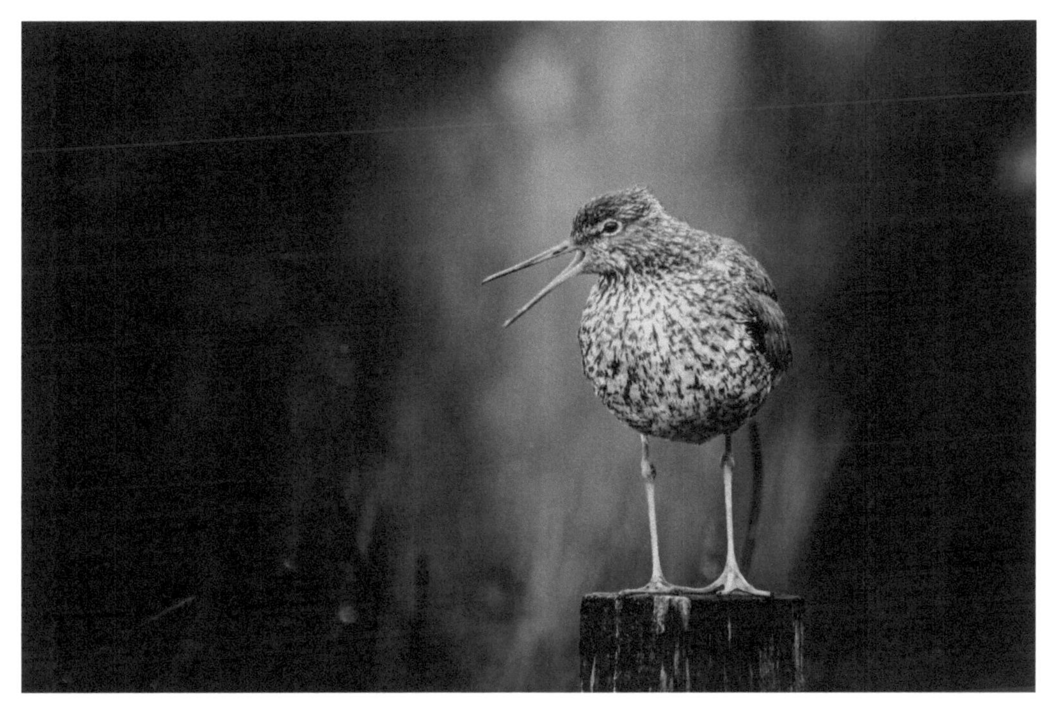

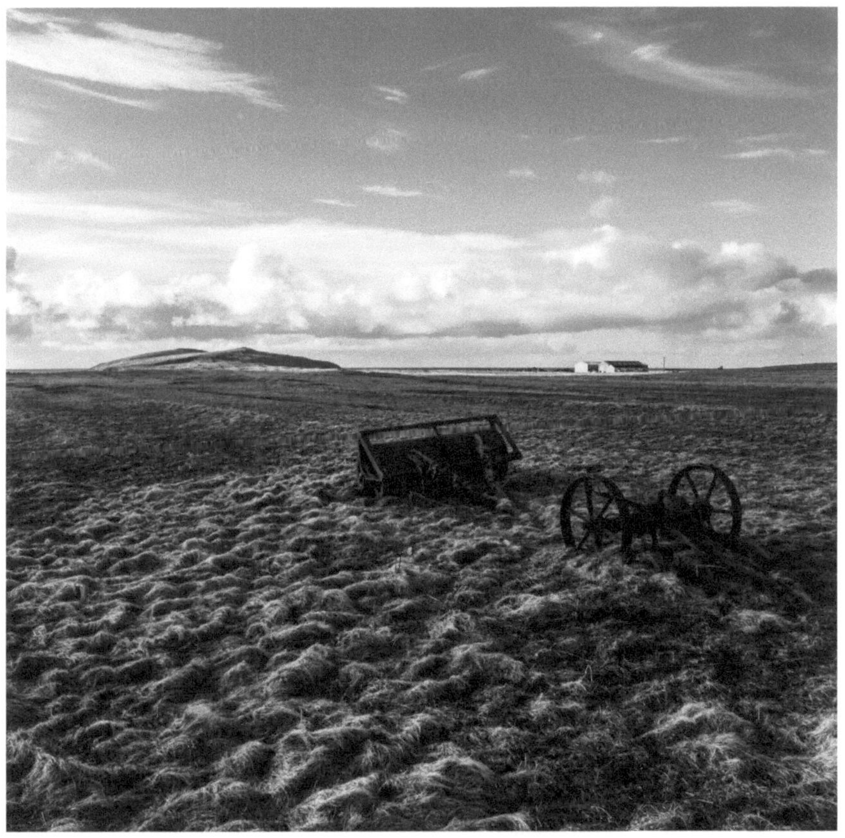

silver and gold—orchids and cornflowers,
birds-foot trefoil, daisies, clover, corn marigold.
The scuts of conies vanish down sand-chutes
and dunlin drag disingenuous broken wings.
Quail crawl through the bent like whistling field mice.
From halfway across the machair—between the abandoned
burial ground and the gutted net station—
the island rises from the swell like Surt.
I can feel the shush and thump of ocean,
breathe the beach's warm kelp breeze.
Patrolling herring gulls monitor my approach
and gannets plunge from the sky's high tower—
then the wind's in my face on the low dunes' ridge,
and there, beyond the precarious, hop-across causeway,
the storm-ripped ruin of An Doirlinn and the crab boats'
wedge of white van landing—twin-papped, raven-crested
Orasaigh stands on its strand before me.

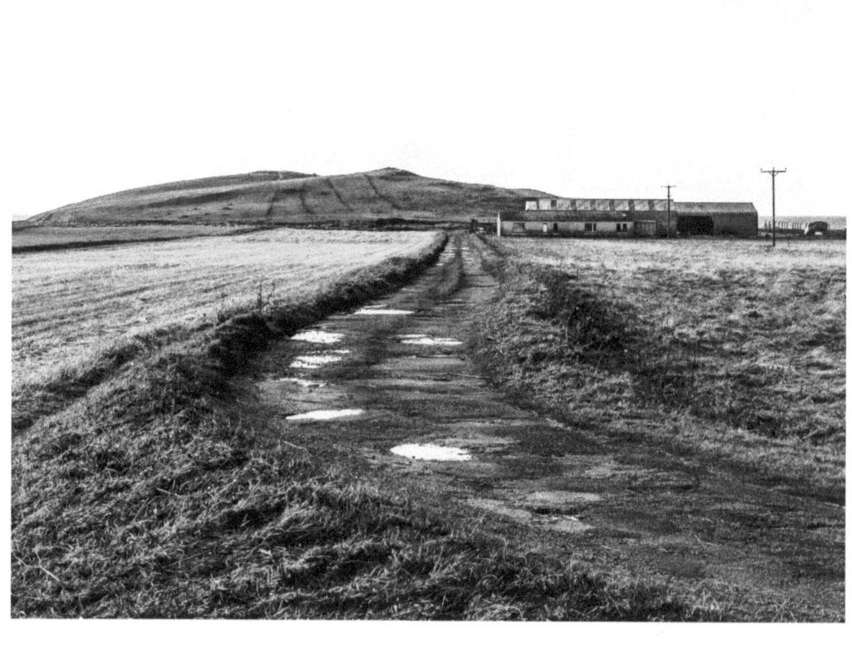

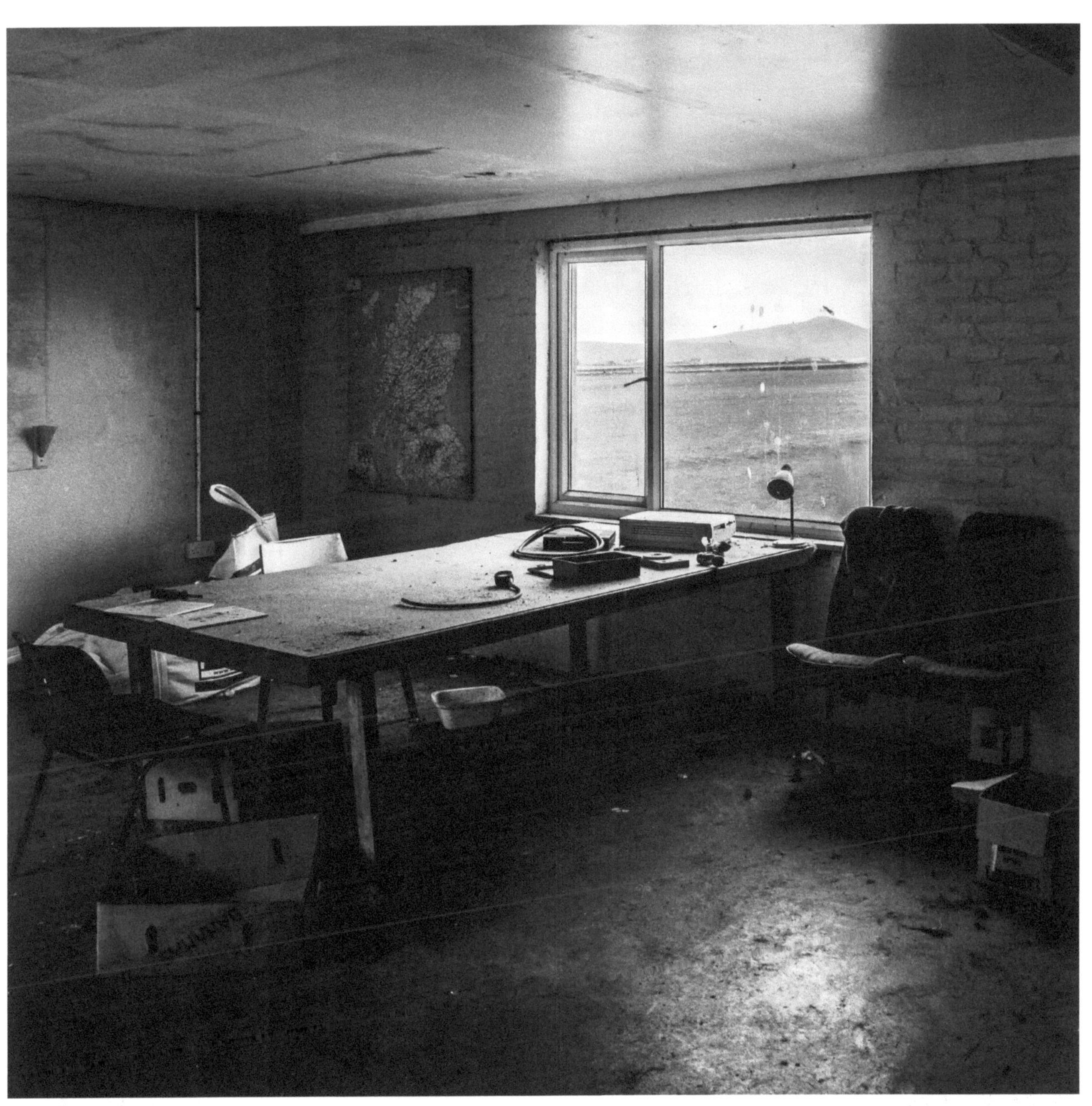

III

Low tide. I pick my way between wrack-matted boulders
and banks of rotting kelp to the storm-gouged gate
to the island. Turf sags above the sand-cliff,
the edge of collapse. A brace of shelduck
bob out on the heave, ducklings strung
like rosary beads between them. Weather-wrecked
stump posts, damp plateau of cotton-grass,
silverweed, bent. Corncrake crexing from the iris beds,
scissor-billed oystercatchers bombing and screaming.
Neolithic, Bronze Age or Pictish stones rise from the turf
like curious seals and note my bold approach.
I climb the slope to the Big Top summit
in the stripes of the evening sun's relief:
sheep paths, turf-sunk boundary walls, run-rig shadows
of long-abandoned plough. Great black-backed gulls
and ravens, circling overhead; one predatory,
the other wary. *Cronk.* Twin peaks, a rushy cleft
between. Exposed gneiss, a tumbled fank
(or dun, or bothy). Each peak is crowned
by a wild-stone menhir: to the south a summit-slipped
altar stone reclines on the wind-cropped turf;
the dorsal fin of a great white shark breaks
the moat of the north peak's sacred pool—
agitated pipits, windy crescendos of towering larks.
The high ground's wide panopticon—due west,
four thousand miles of ocean, the calves of Saglek Bay.
To the east, the cloud-capped, herded hills
of Stùlabhal, Easabhal, Chionnich.
The toytown townlands spread before me
along the Viking shore—Cille Pheadair, Baghasdail,
Leth Meadhanach, Smercleit, Geàrraidh na Mònadh;

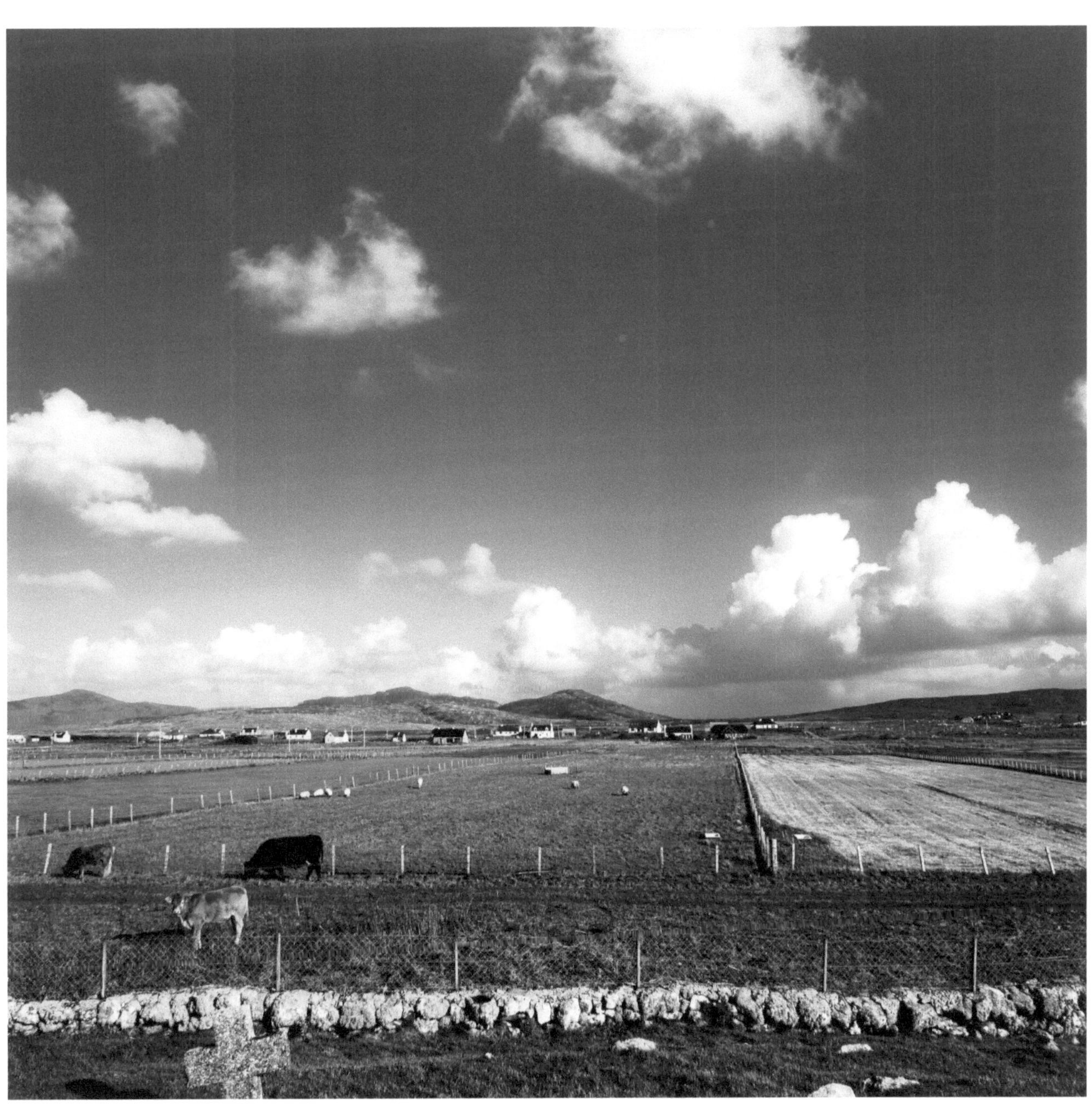

white horses of Eriskay, blue hills of Barra beyond.
The back of the island slopes down to its hunkered cliffs.
Wave-hewn riprap, tide-heaved tethers of kelp.
Great northern divers ride the waves, on their summer cruise
to Iceland. Cormorants, mocking the crucifixion.
On the topmost ledge of a storm-gouged cove,
a shit-fligged heap of kelp; a family of ravens,
aloft above the menhirs. Fulmars cut the sunlit slope's
bright spindrift—one summer I fell asleep here,
and had to wade to land: otter breaking from its flounder,
disbelieving. I drop to the path above the rocks
looking north along Tràigh na Doirlinn. Jewels glinting
in the grass: primrose, violet, tormentil.
Sentinel oystercatchers, incessant and ubiquitous,
their piping alarums ripped off on incessant,
ubiquitous wind. Crab boat anchored in the headland's lee,
where the Northmen dragged their longboats
up on to the sandy haven. Ringed plover tight
on the driftwood strandline. Wind-wrecked fence post.
Turf sags above the sand-cliff. I pick my way
between wrack-matted boulders and banks of rotting kelp
to the storm-gouged gate to the island.

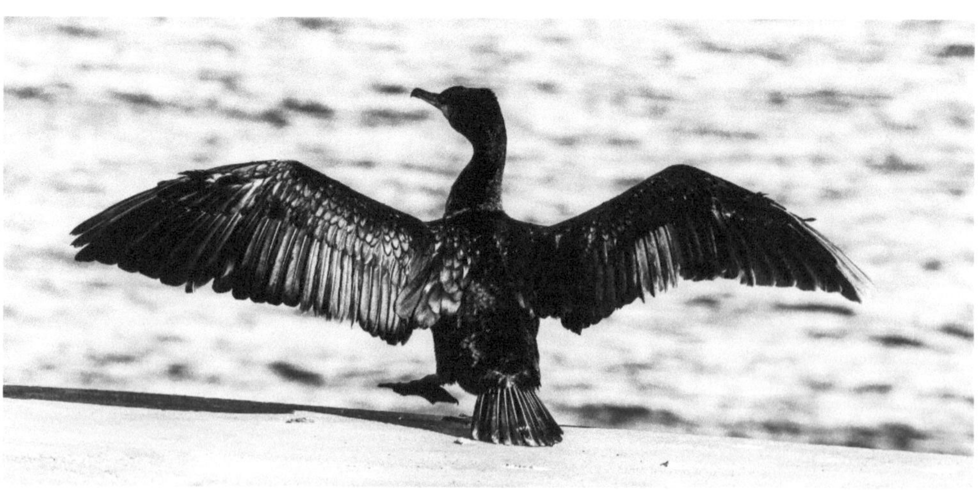

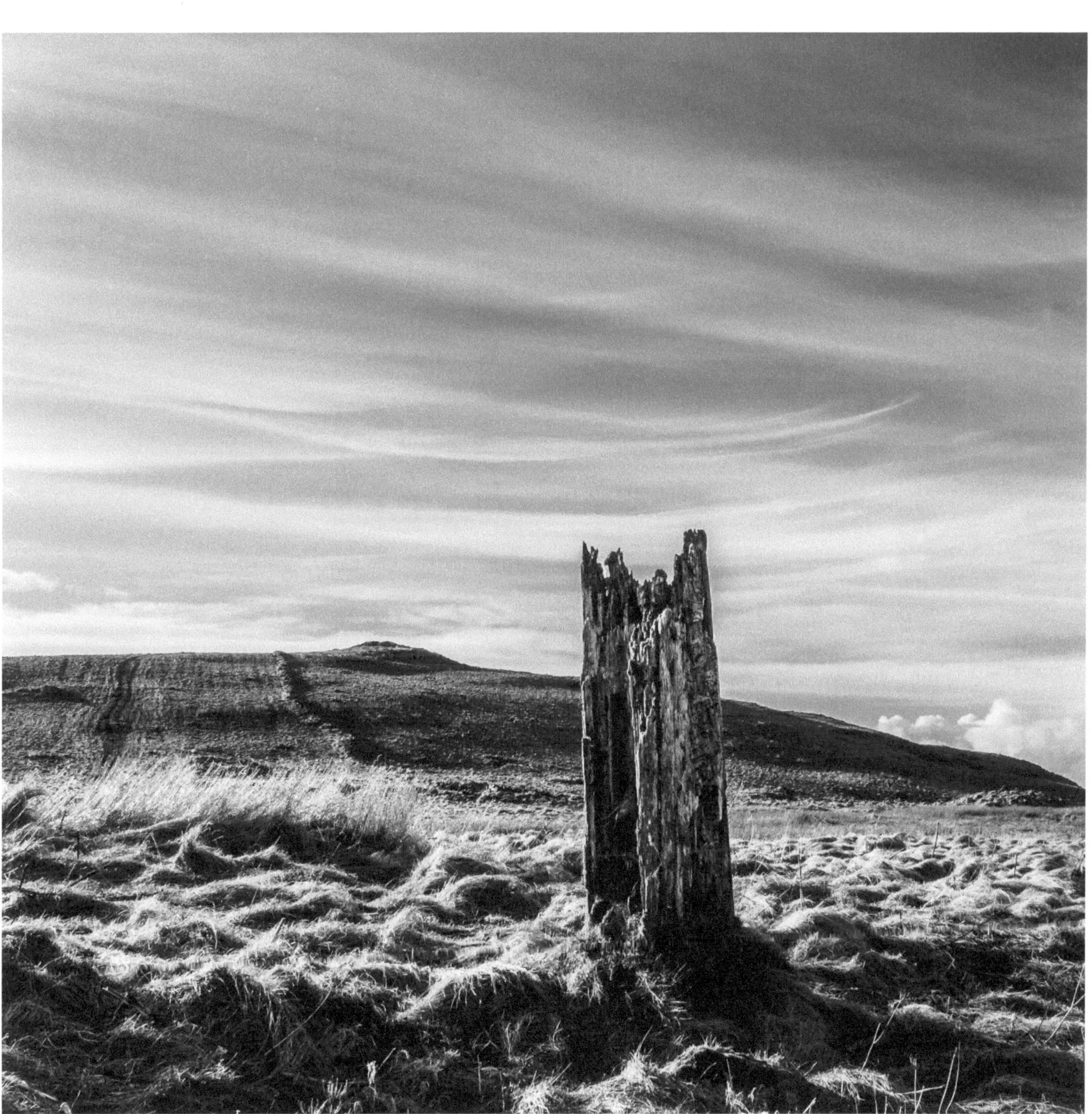

AN DOIRLINN

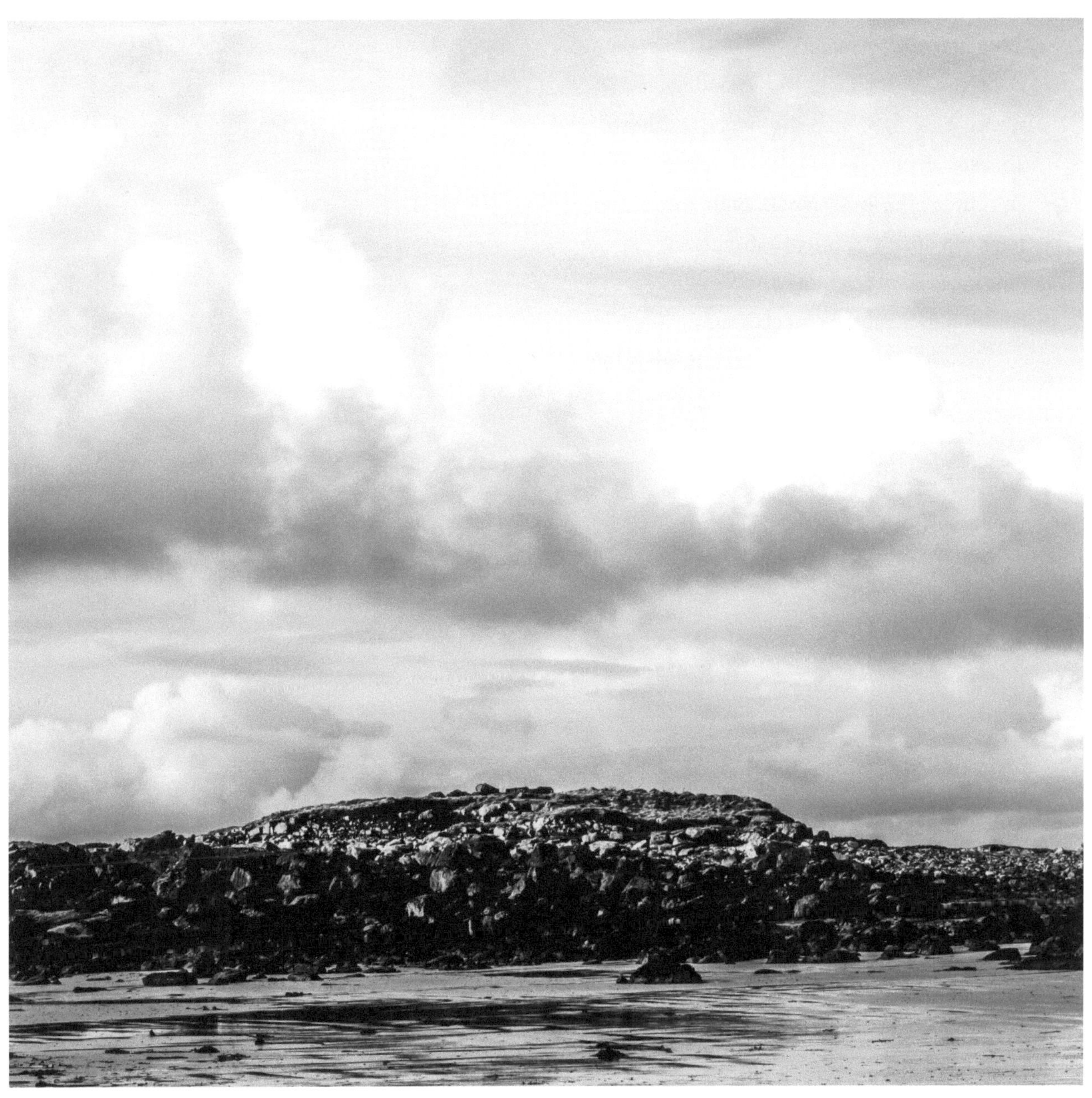

I

Isthmus, peninsula, tombolo, spit.
'Landing' derived from usage—snekkja,
bìrlinn, sgoth. A blue-ringed tidal-islet,
the shape of a guillemot's egg—731174,
OS Explorer 453. Causewayed landing,
stacks of creels. Crab boats moored offshore.
That smash of rocks and ripped-up turf
en-route to the lovely island. Built, low-walled,
but not a dun: the cyclone's disgorged
flint-knap scatter bespoke the Neolithic,
confirmed by subsequent excavation:
successive layers of occupation, 3,700 to 2,400 B.C.

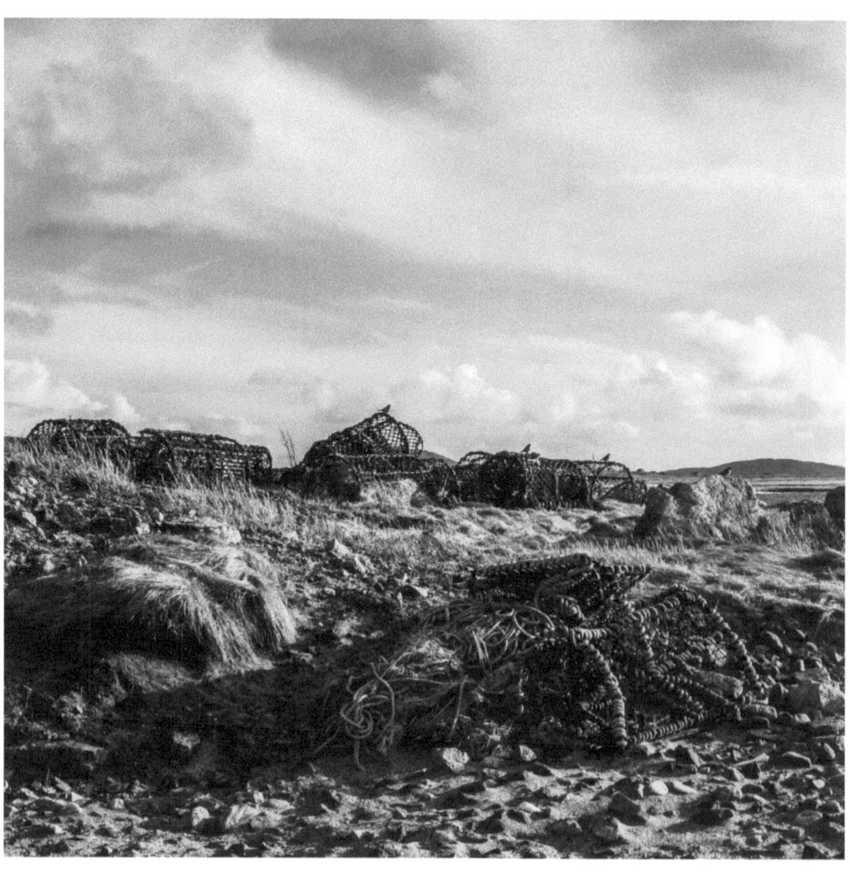

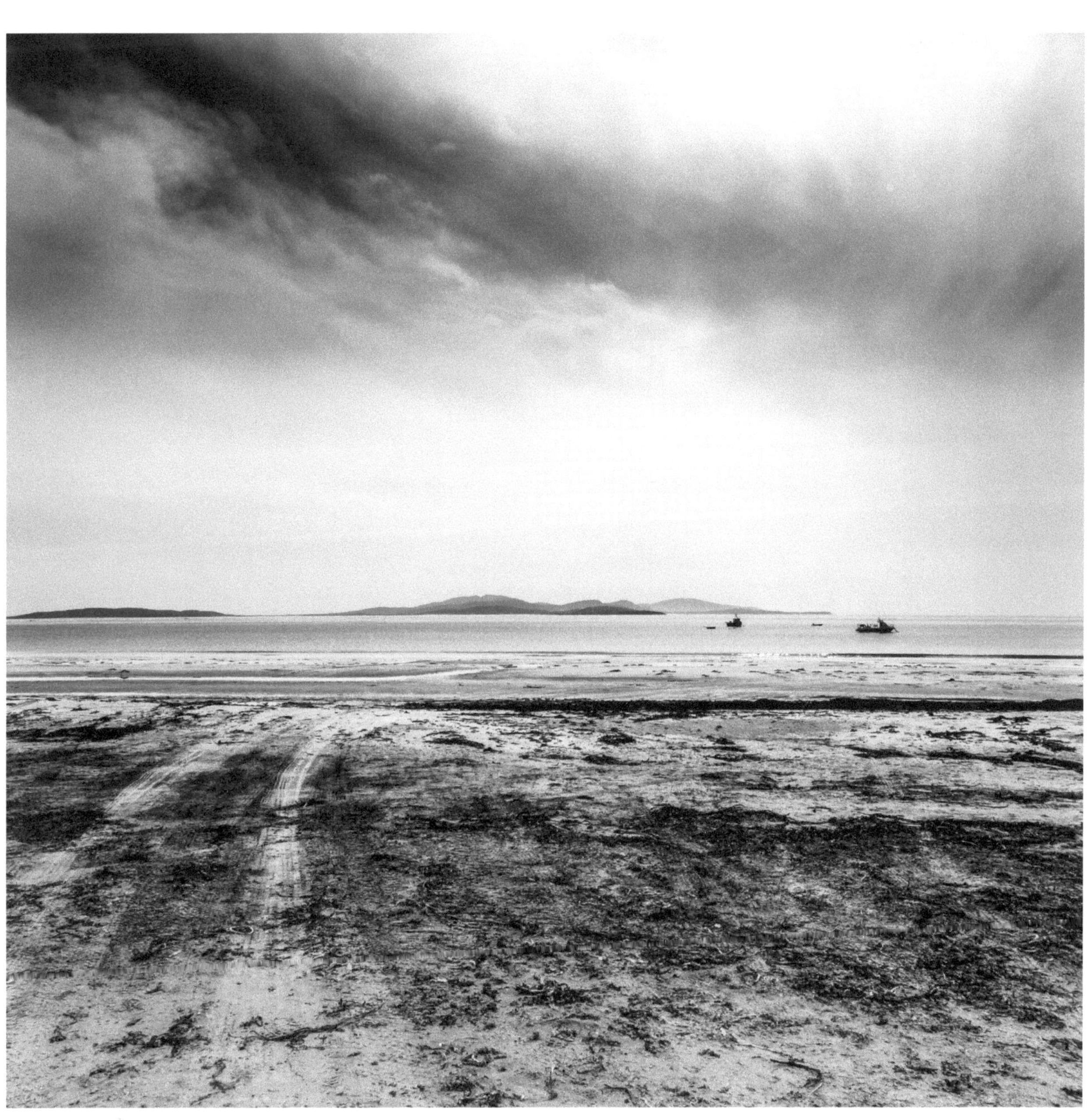

II

When Scorpion II was lord in Nekhen
and Gilgamesh reigned in Uruk,
the farmers of Boisdale had been turning the sod
for half a thousand years—trumpeting mammoths
on Wrangel Island, sea cows roaming the plains of kelp
from Pribilof to Lewis—picked bones of garefowl
dumped on middens for the next five thousand years.
The steading no *doirlinn*, but a bump at the foot
of the westernmost hill in the forest of Uist,
the land-devouring ocean still a mile or more due west.
Clearing the woodland, burning back scrub;
scratching furrows between the stumps for emmer
and six-rowed bere. Aurochsen, deer and Irish elk,
gone to the dogs. Canis familiaris. Wolf and bear
to the bottom of the Minch, with the cachalots
and right whales. Paddocks for ovis, sus and bos.
Material culture: stone walls, stone hearths, stone axes;
a flaked-flint knife, smashed carinated pottery.
No hieroglyph or baked clay tablet, painted tomb
or bas-relief. Archaeological speculations
built on scant empirical altars: bloodstone bigshots
cornering the surplus, investing in astronomical
priesthoods and vernacular death-mitigation schemes:
seven days and nights I wept for my brother
until the worms of Enlil fastened in his flesh.
Deadly theatre of ritual landscape; flint arrowheads
signifying war. They mated with pigs and chapped-face children,
killed strangers for profit and neighbours in fits of rage.
In times of dearth they starved the old codgers
and fed their shrunken wreckage to the dogs.
They lived at one with Magna Mater, dug henbane beer
and Aqualung. DNA says, *they're just like us—*
undestroyable serpopard, sphinx that moves the sun!
In his house beneath the ocean, Great Kraken lies waiting.

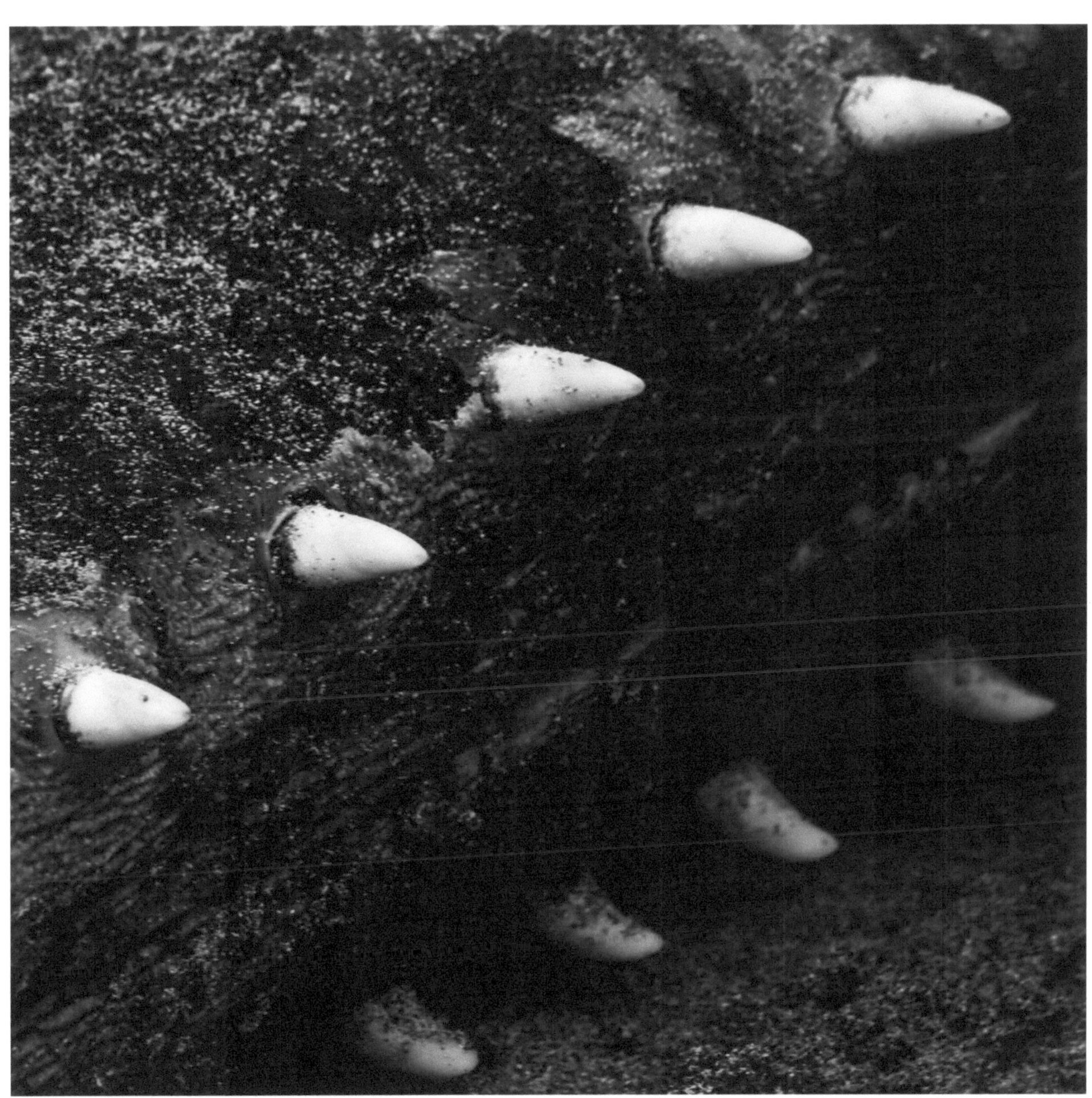

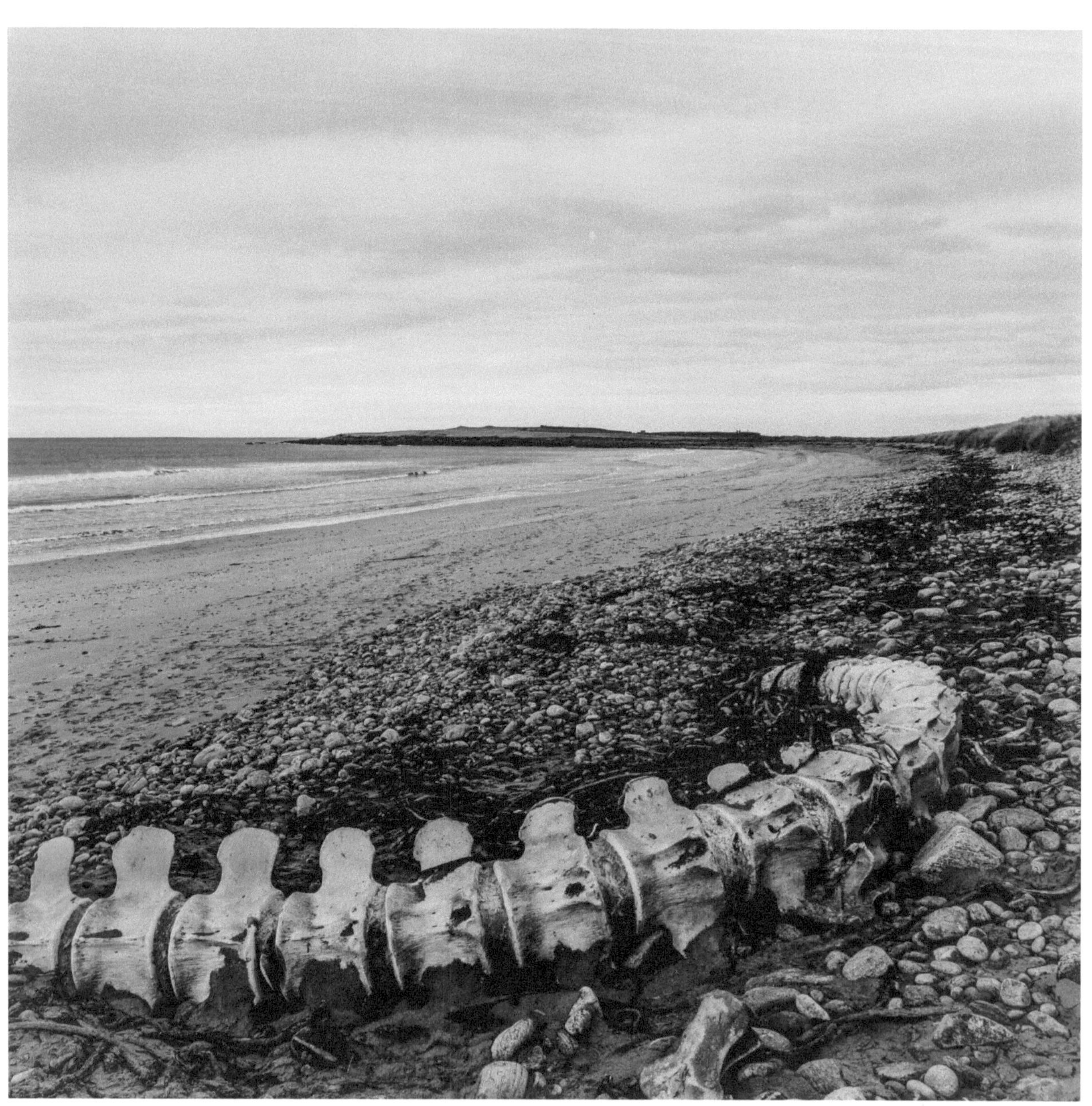

III

A great black-backed gull labours aloft
from the rocks below the turf-scabbed mound.
She's been tugging the guts from a washed-up
porpoise, snagged beneath the wall. She settles
on the strand of Tràigh na Doirlinn to watch me
prod and probe. Zip of grinning peg-teeth.
Eye-socket caves and jailhouse window ribcage.
Tangle-stink of nacreous intestines.
This beach is good for the wreckers of dead cetaceans,
the scavengers and collectors: the lumbar vertebrae
of a pothead blackfish, somewhere in the shed;
the mandible blades of a minke whale,
lost to the tides or a rival necrophiliac
when I dallied too long at the Polochar Inn;
the digital image of the Risso's dolphin, torn open
and wolfed by a slaughter of gleeful ravens.
What else does the kindly ocean bring?
Mary's Nut, Sea Purse, sixty-foot trunks
of shock-root loblolly pine; skraelings stitched
into buckskin thongs, unravelling bark canoes.
Puffins, seals and narwhals. A case of Spey Royal.
A naked lady with bitten-off fingers
washed up from Tràigh Siar. Cluny's man had her rings.
Una had her frock. The black-backed gull
had the pearls that were her eyes.
Bowed heads around a gaping lozenge of sand:
hunc tumulum benedicere dignare, eique
Angelum tuum sanctum deputa custodem.
The resurrection and the life. The kindness
of strangers in their threadbare Sunday best.
He took it all—their land, their livings, the shirts
off their humped and weal-encrusted backs.

IV

Surf breaks on Tràigh na Doirlinn and rushes
up the beachface. Clockwork sanderling
switchback in the swash-zone like speeded up footage
from a silent film, picking tiny titbits
from the foam. They're fuelling up for Iceland
and Franz Josef Land beyond, the ever-receding
Arctic edge of the Holocene interglacial.
A whippet flies in and the sanderling lift and scatter,
flashing twittering chevrons down the beach
towards the headland at Cille Pheadair.
Uprush wipes their footprints' blurred cuneiform.
How many billion sanderling have stopped-off here,
since ice-melt stretched the north from Spain?
Where are their embalmed, mummified corpses,
their stelae in the foam's wet sand?
Scorpion left his mark: his skull-crushing mace
and gibbet of lapwings. Gilgamesh cleared
the sacred groves from ocean to Euphrates.
He slew the lion, glorying in life, hyena,
stag and panther. All manner of small game.
He butchered the mighty Bull of Heaven
and fed its heart to Shamash. His swastika
wheels from Göbekli Tepe to the trenches
of the western ocean, its cargo of infinite dead.
A Sailor of the 1939-1945 War,
Merchant Navy. Buried 21st August, 1940.
The pharaohs of Cluny, Westminster, Wannsee.
The dead go into the Sun. Ice-melt washes
their genocides clean. Atlantic ripping away.

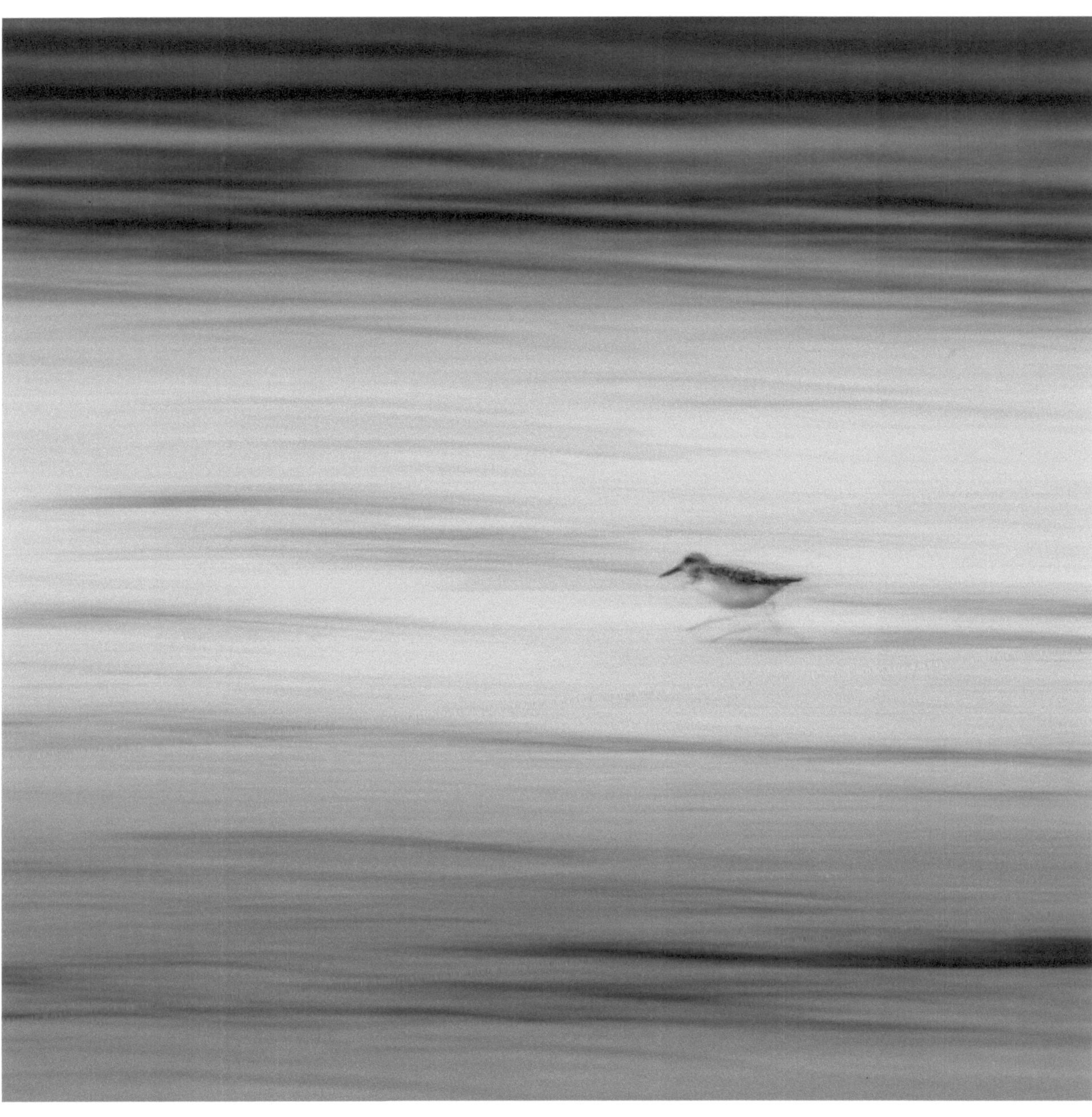

THE STONES

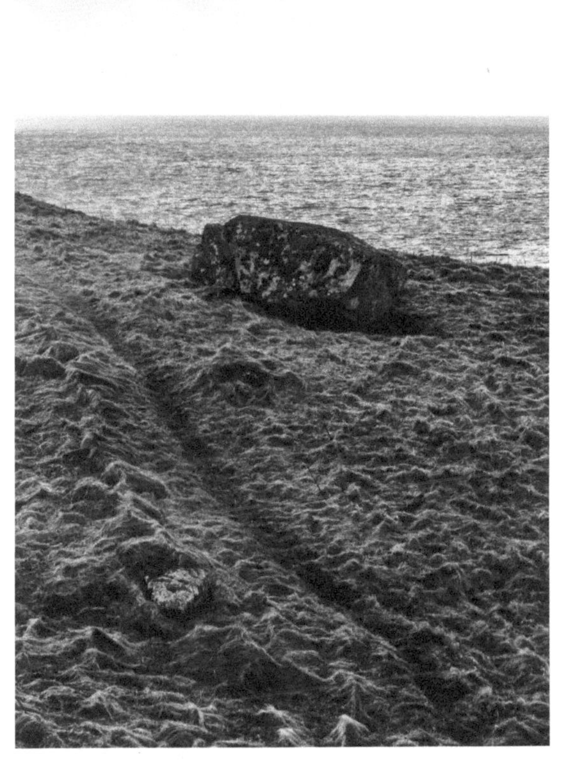

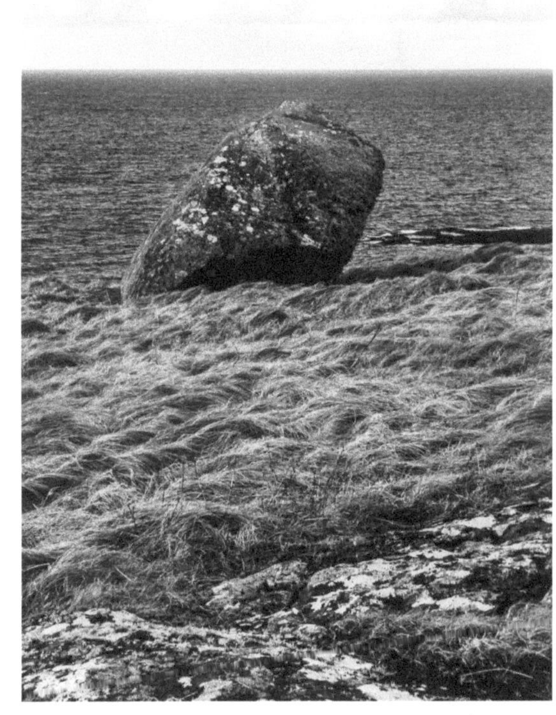

I

Up the grassy hvalsbak to the cleft
between the paps, each low mound nippled
in its slipped, off-centre stone: a tumbled altar,
the dorsal fin of a basking shark.
Three billion years old Lewisian gneiss,
rough concrete hide of an Indian elephant:
grey quartz, underglint pinks of mica.
The southern peak's sacrificial stone,
recumbent under the threadbare summit
and sheltered from the salt Atlantic,
is scabbed in moss and yellow croton,
sea ivory's shaggy wintergreen.
The north peak's upright jag of fang
is scoured to the stone on the windward side
and streaked in the shites of ravens.
Bumfluff ramalina furs the underlean of lee.

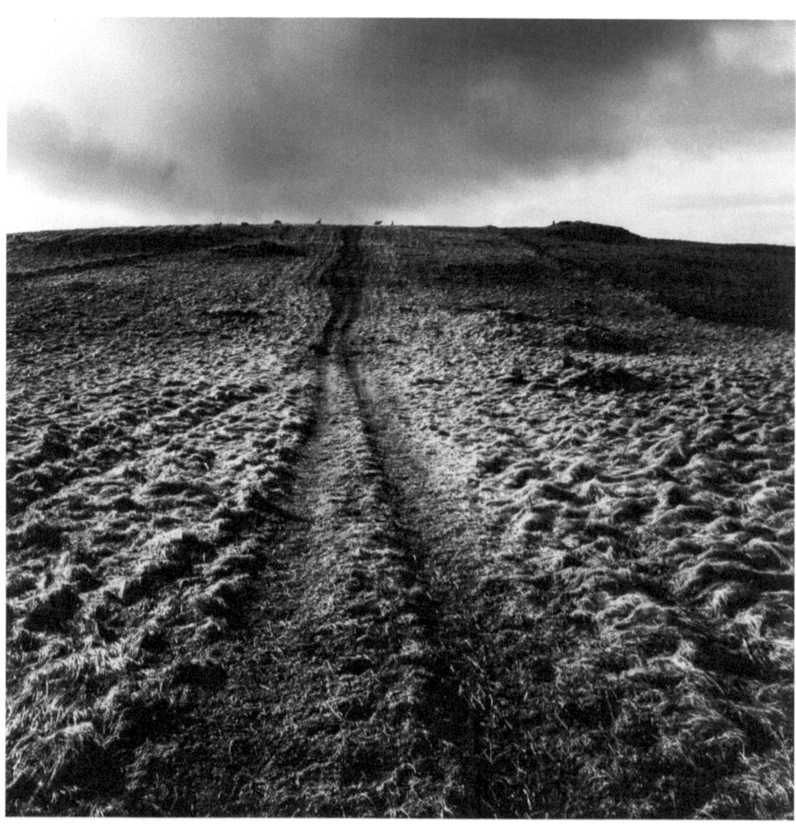

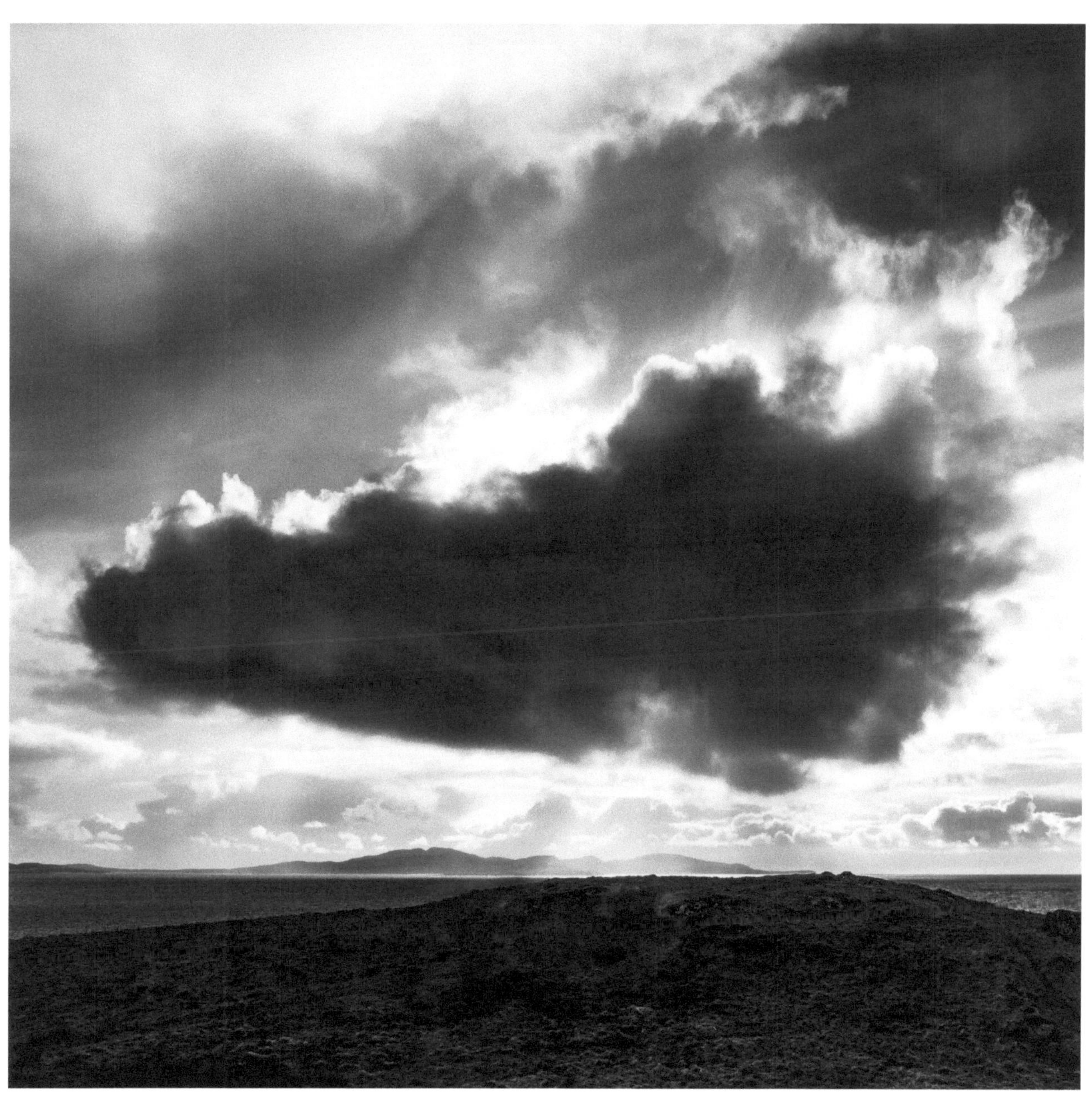

II

Mike Parker Pearson calls Orasaigh's stones
spontaneous megaliths; natural features,
that to the novice or self-deluding,
suggest a Stonehenge hand—blame Baldrick
or the Modern Antiquarian. I defer, of course,
but looking three-sixty from Orasaigh's summit
it's hard to believe that this grassy ziggurat—
the highest prominence on the plain of Uist
from Rubha Hornais to Ceann a' Ghàraidh—
didn't rise above Doirlinn's Neolithic quotidian
to quicken in peoples' dreams. Now, as surely then,
the landscape knits together from the vantage
of its summit. Open your arms, and embrace
the evening sun. For the hundred and twenty degrees
of your span, all you can see is the squinting gold of ocean:
sun-swallower, storm-bringer, bearer of bounty,
edge of the knowable world. Due north is the foam-fringed
diamond-head of Rubha Àird a' Mhuile, ground further down
on its sea-level stump with every passing year.
To the south, across her horse-plunged sound,
spreads womanly Barra, the cleft between Heabhal
and Hartabhul, mirroring Orasaigh's own.
A bead drawn roughly east-north-east takes the eye
through the clefted rifle sights of Càireasbhal's
microcosmic stones, and beyond to the cleave
of Coire na Cuilc, between many-breasted
Triuirebheinn and Choinnich. The chambered tomb
of Trosaraidh, a clear mile east-south-east;
the chambered tomb of Layaval, a clear mile
south-south-east. The standing stone at Pol a' Charra.
Bones ripped from the kists at storm-torn

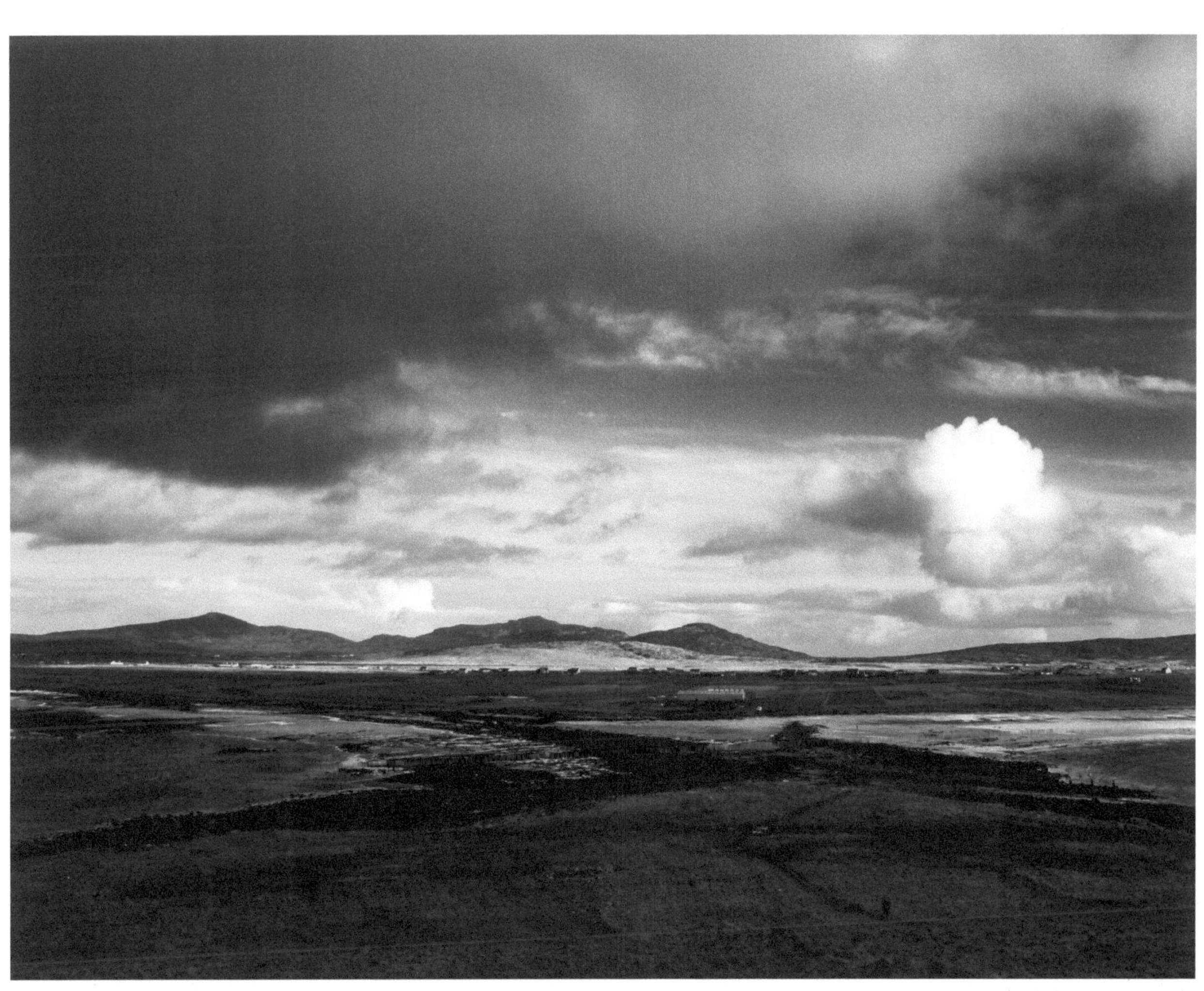

Ceann a' Ghàraidh. Atlantic hurricanes,
lightning strikes, aurora borealis. Hyperborean
winter darkness over fields of freezing peat.
Hesperidean summer light over plains of shimmering bere.
The cloud-commanding anvil-tops of Thacla,
Choradail, Mhòr. The eagle and the aurochs
and the curragh-capsizing whale. The pounce of death:
stone axe, droch shùil, the body-blotching fever,
breath sucked from your ribcage in the night.
A people thrown on the littoral edge,
making sense of it somehow, encoding land
with dream and meaning, the seer's inaccessible vision—
'a semiotic landscape of the living and the dead'.
Niall Sharples, Neil Oliver, Mike Parker Pearson.
I heckle the telly and think I know best.
Blame Baldrick and the Modern Antiquarian.

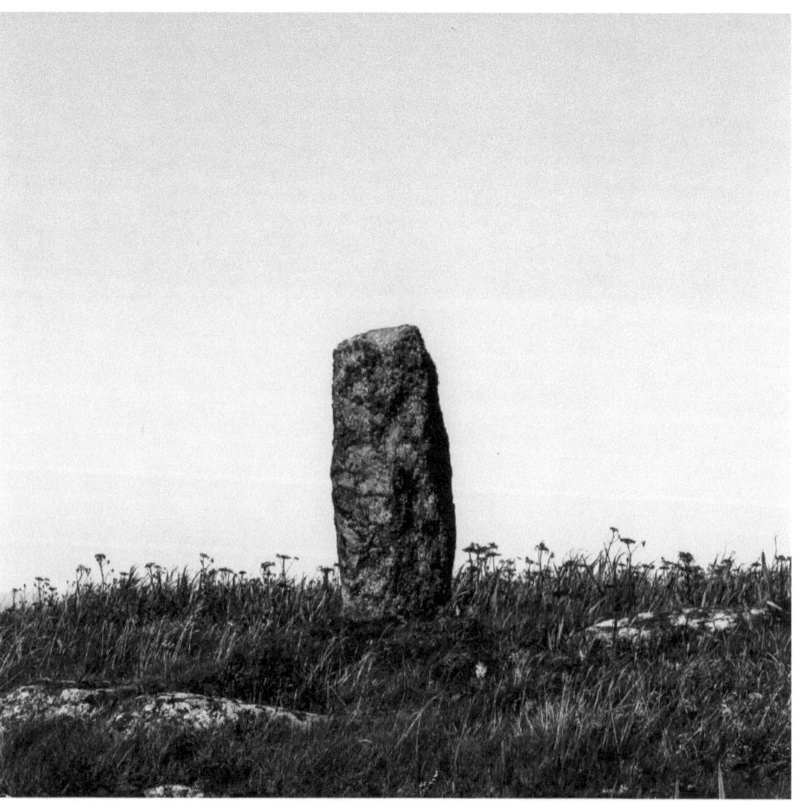

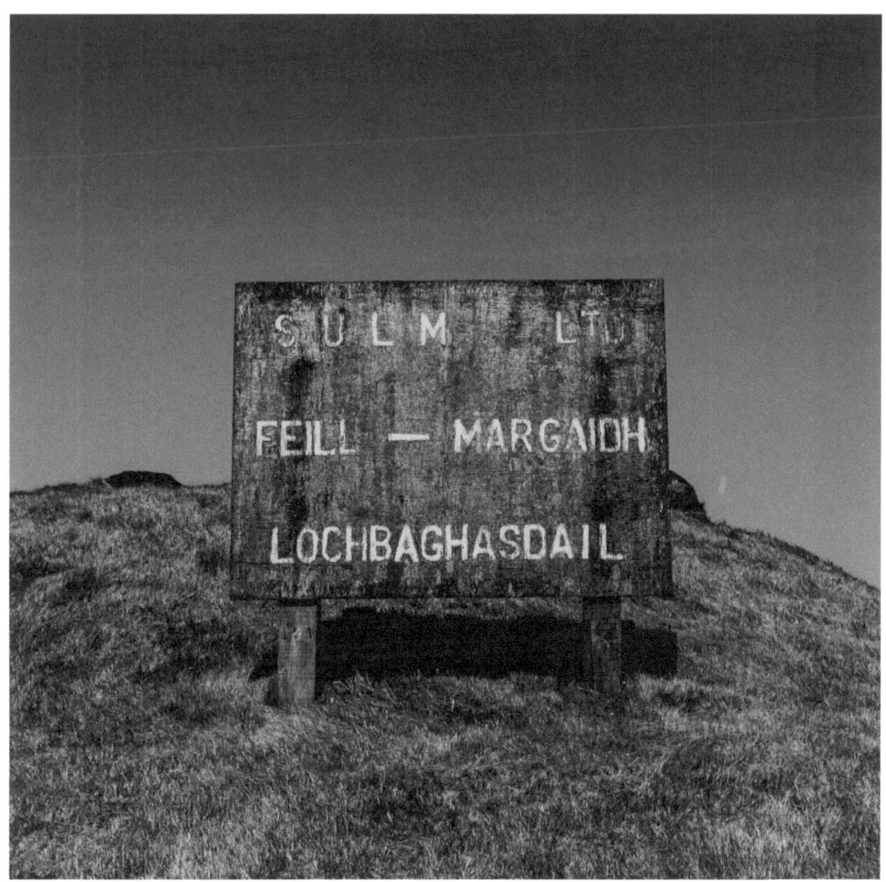

III

I came here of my own free will, bearing
the orb and sceptre of my yearning and ambition.
I tossed my seed like pearls upon the earth.
Cracked gags like a condemned hysteric.
I fitted the bill alright. But the sun was shining,
and a cuckoo bounced its echo off the rocks.
I gathered armfuls of flag in a meadow of farting shorthorns
and led off a lamb with my thumb in its mouth.
These things made me smile. But the cuckoo
just wouldn't stop bouncing its echo, the flag went over
and the lamb went to market in a livestock trailer.
I came across a cormorant, nailed to a squat, low rock.
Piteous bleating. Oh God. Oh Jesus Christ.

IV

Gavin Maxwell, machine-gunning basking sharks
like some silver-spoon Quint. You know his type—
a dilettante playboy from the minor nobility,
freed by trusts and networks of blood
from the need to earn a living. A 'free spirit',
macho and moody, otherworldly, and a bit of a
NATURE MYSTIC, owning islands, otters and servants.
Groupies including Italian Vogue, Kath Raine
and Terry Nutkins; congeners including John Aspinall,
Mubarak bin London and the Price of Whales—
the Prince of Gaels? Lucan gone to ground
on Eilean Bàn with the otter that bit off
the Nutty Boy's fingers. Deer, grouse, salmon.
Sirs, Lordships, Majesties. Their ever-so-lovely
or brown-teethed Ladies. Their men, their *little men*,
their *servants*: ghillies and gamekeepers, crofters
and kelpers—trash for the garbage-boat passage
to Saskatchewan. Resettlement in the west,
aktioned by Union's besporanned *Schottischerrat*:
clearance, plantation and laissez-faire death.
John Broon's body lies a-mouldering in Glencoe,
Jimmy Savile goes noncing on. By Appointment.
Having cleared the Mi'kmaq and the French,
the Baronets of Nova Scotia lorded it over
the destitute Gaels of Hallaig—Connolly
in the khaki of the Irish Citizen Army,
Cornford dead in the cause of Spain.

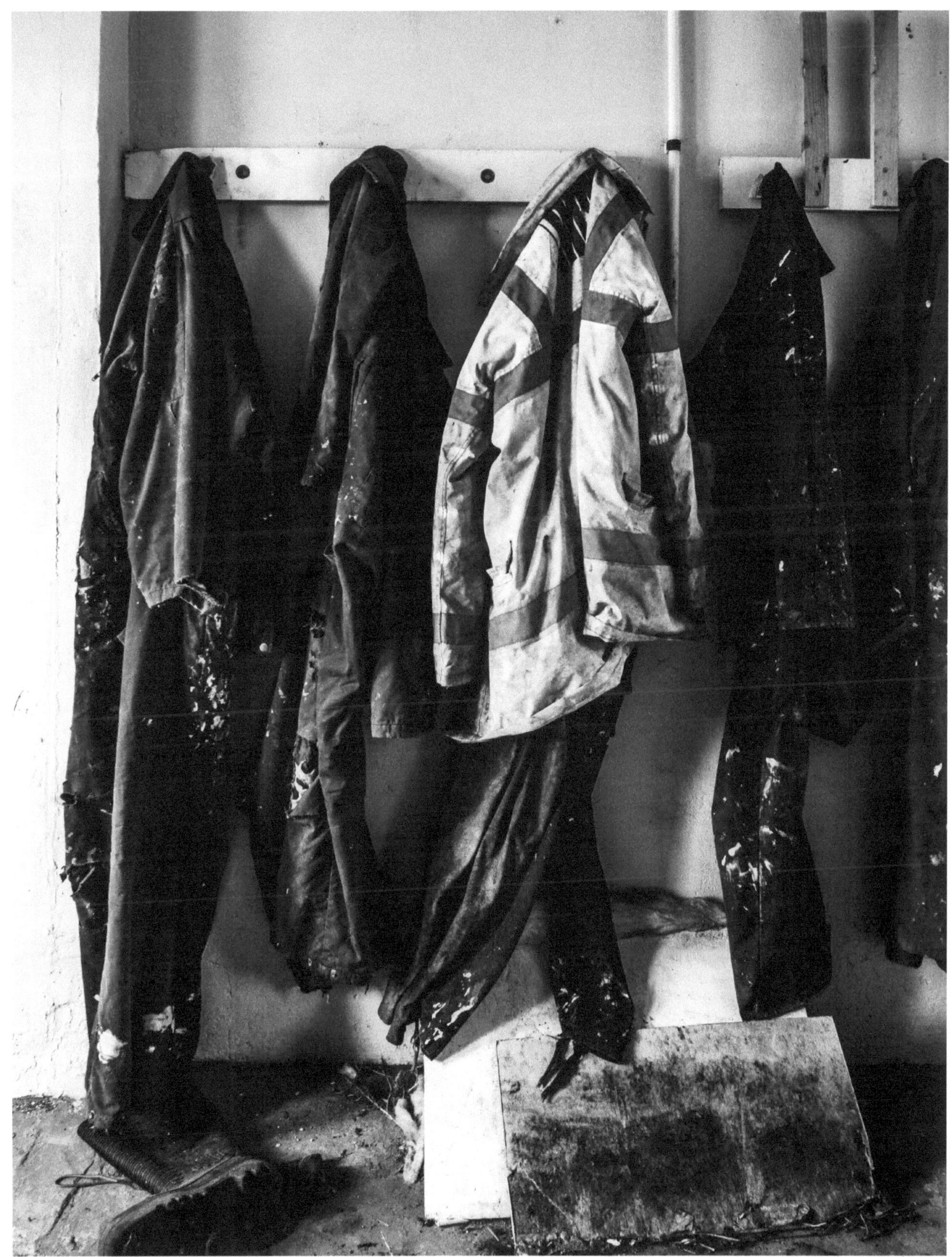

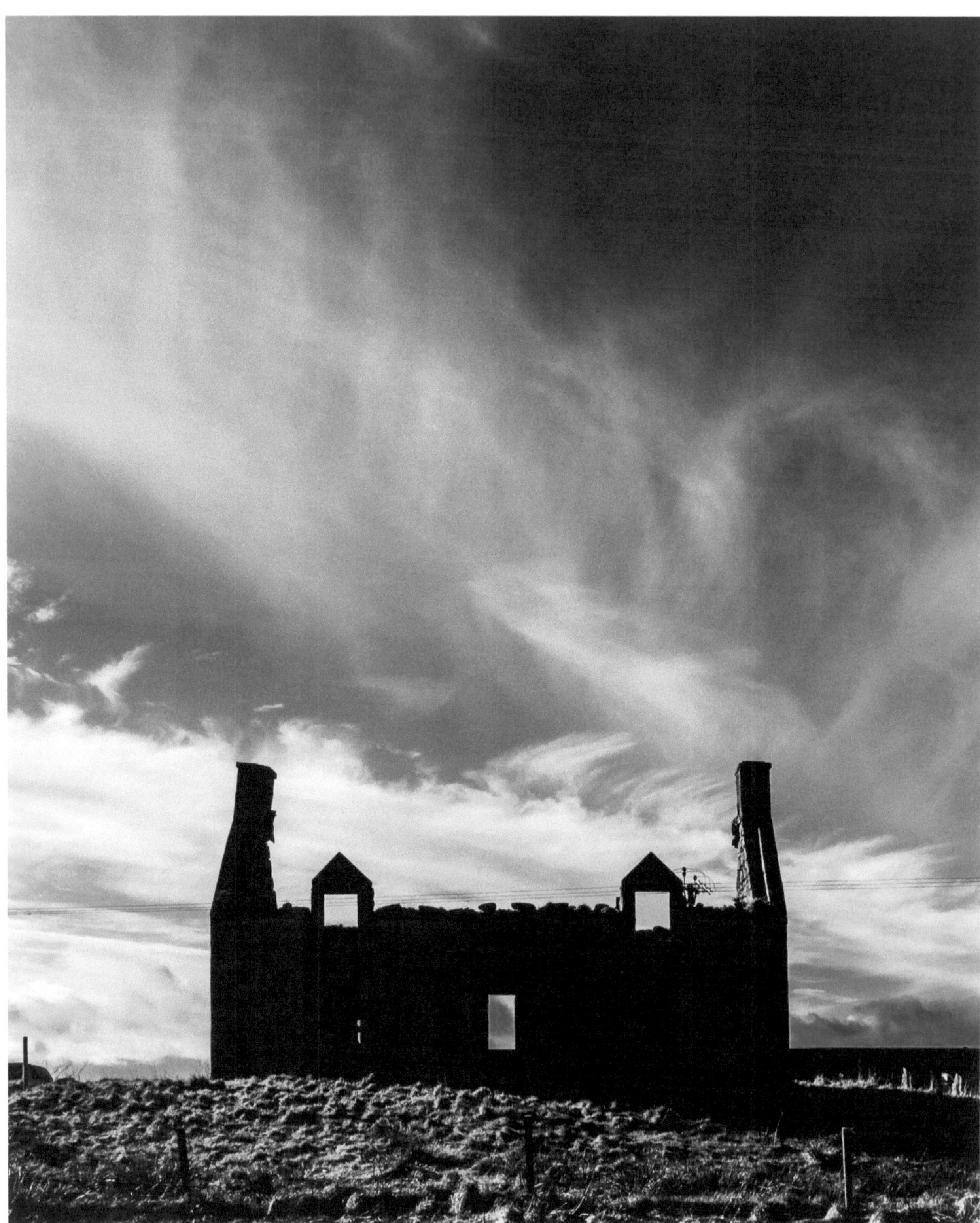

Georgi Dimitrov, five months draped in Nazi chains,
exploding the bluster of the dilettante playboy
at Leipzig. The dorsal fin of a great-white shark,
breaking the blood-red waters of Clyde,
chasing the salmon and sturgeon upstream.
The gravelly redds of Mick McGahey,
broken kelts in the broken reeds, ravaged
by the vermin of the City—a rat race is for rats.
The dorsal fin of a great-white shark, a spectre
haunting Europe and the World. This shark,
swallow you whole. Anyway, I delivered the bomb.

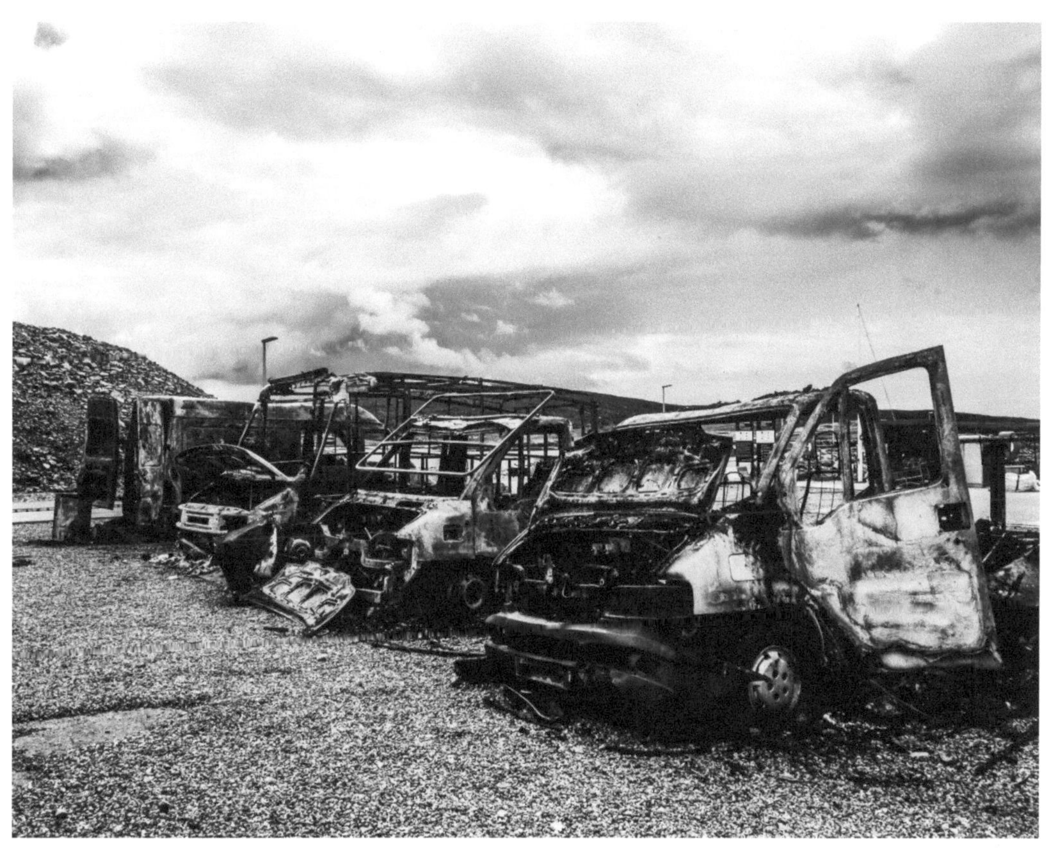

V

I fell asleep beneath the stones in the warmth
of the failing sun. Dreams throbbed
between the pillars of my thermonuclear temples.
Stone axe shattering mussels on the rocks:
brain matter, herring gull screams. Maxwell manuring
his lazybeds with the spraints of young otters—
Terry giving him the finger. The tractor-chugged
golden townlands, the flat-calm bìrlinn's golden seas.
Breið-øx splintering a ribcage on the rocks—ravens
on the altar and shark-fin stones, pulling me apart.

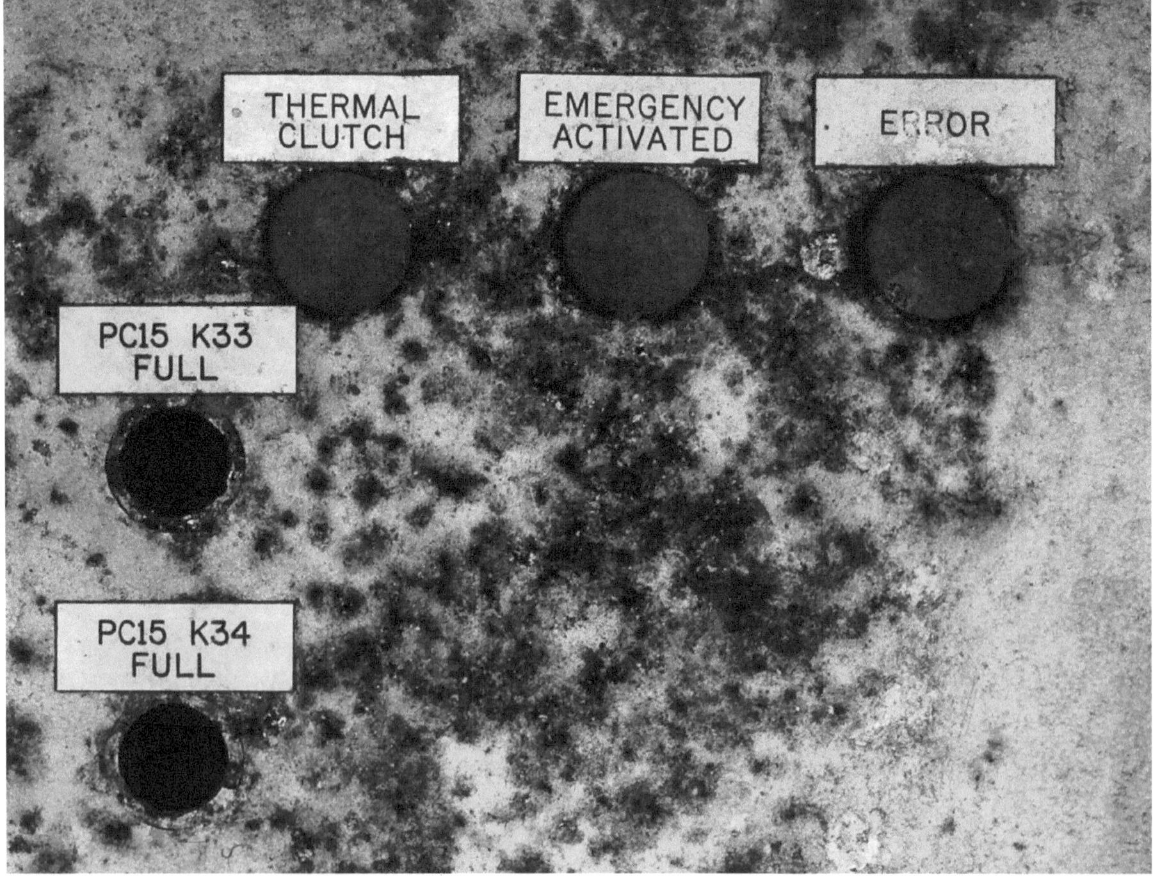

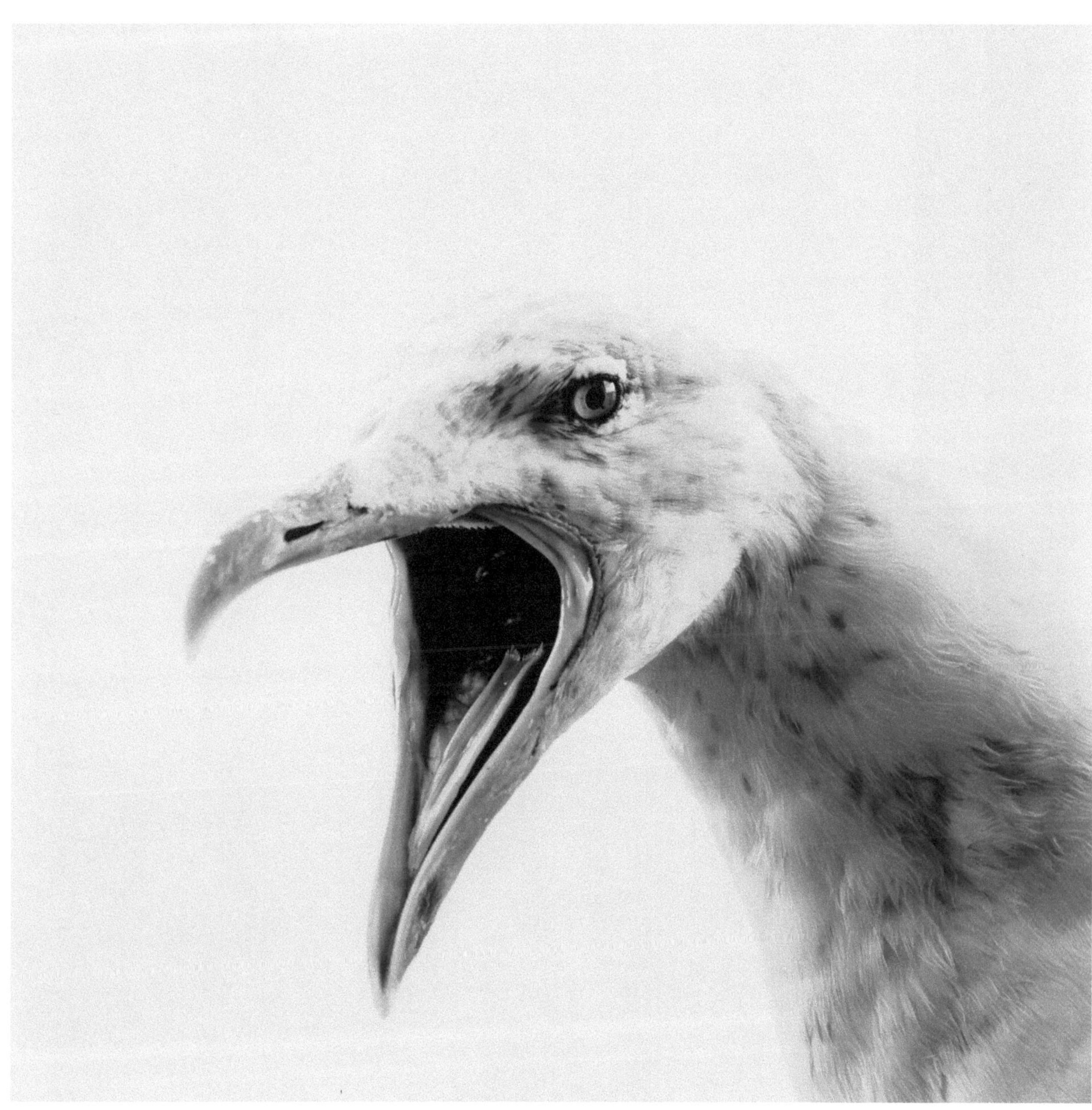

THE RAVEN'S EYRIE

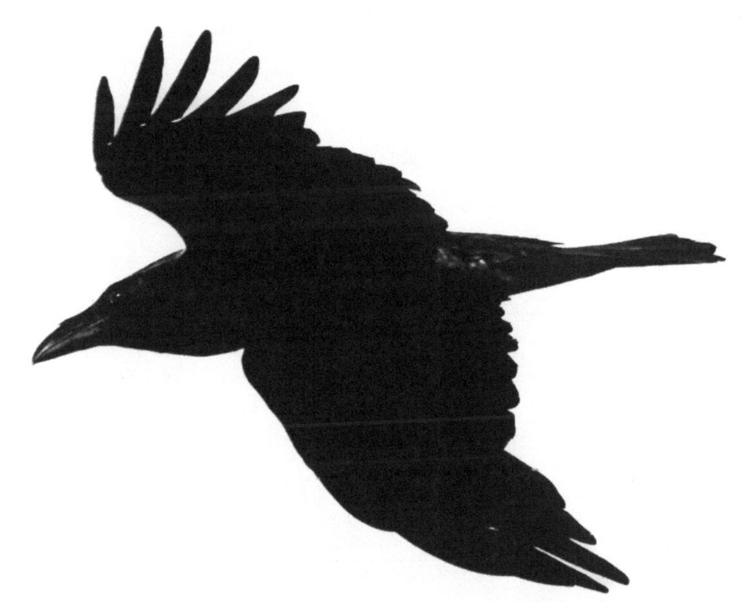

I

Where the island falls away below the shark-fin
stone, Atlantic has gnawed a sheer-backed cove.
On Fair Isle they'd call it a geo—cliffs of gneiss
and gravelly substrate, tussocks of undercut turf.
The back wall drops six fathoms to the beach,
its flotsam of buoys and nylon rope, black wrack
and white, disarticulate sheep. The side walls slope
to the gate of ocean, low tide's suck and slap
of swell. Oystercatchers yelping from the rocks;
herring gulls drifting over; a convoy of cormorants,
bound for the Sound of Barra. Under the turf-lip,
a man's height down, a pad of kelp and felted fleece.
Squirts of white emulsion. The ledge it rests on
is an ibex path. If you hold your nerve you can walk it.

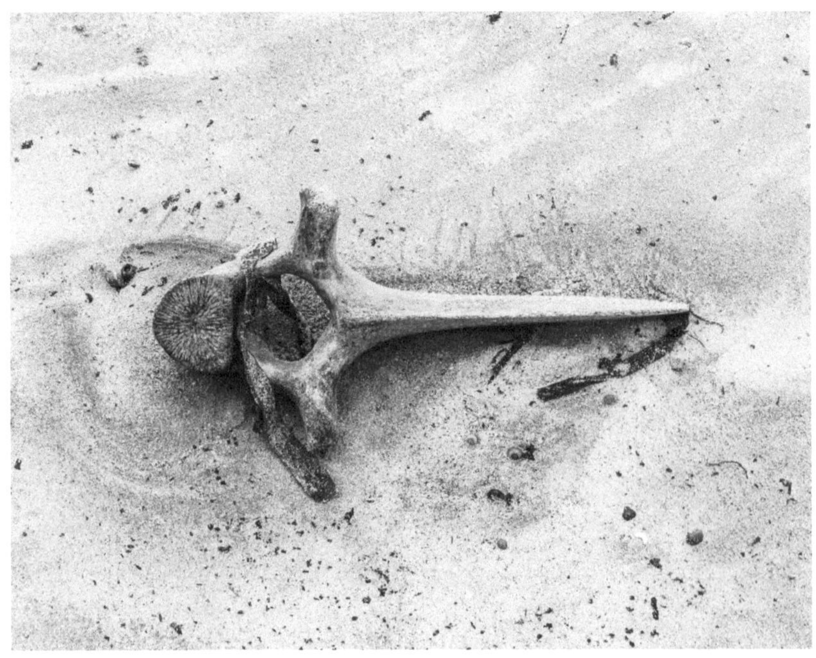

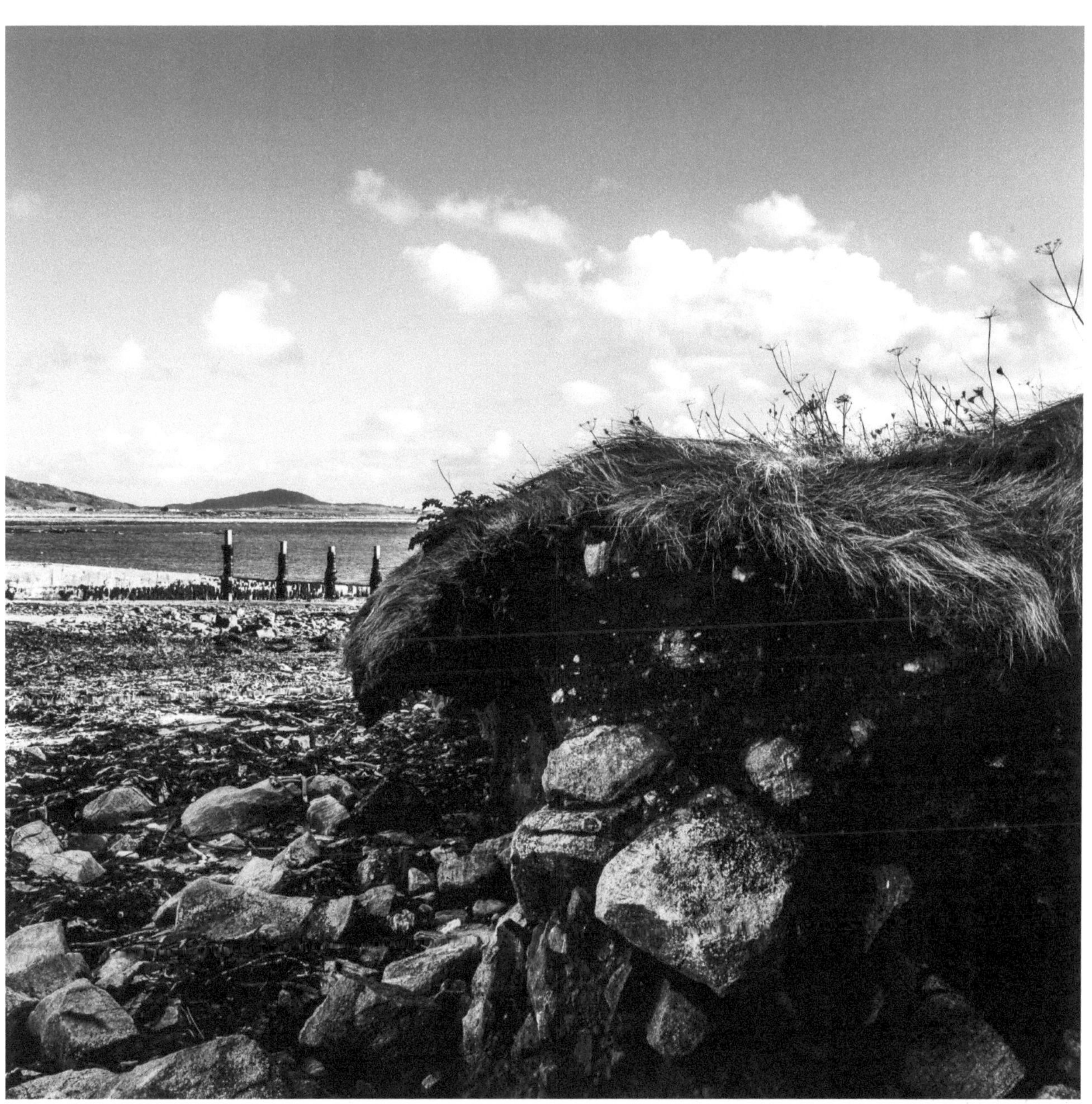

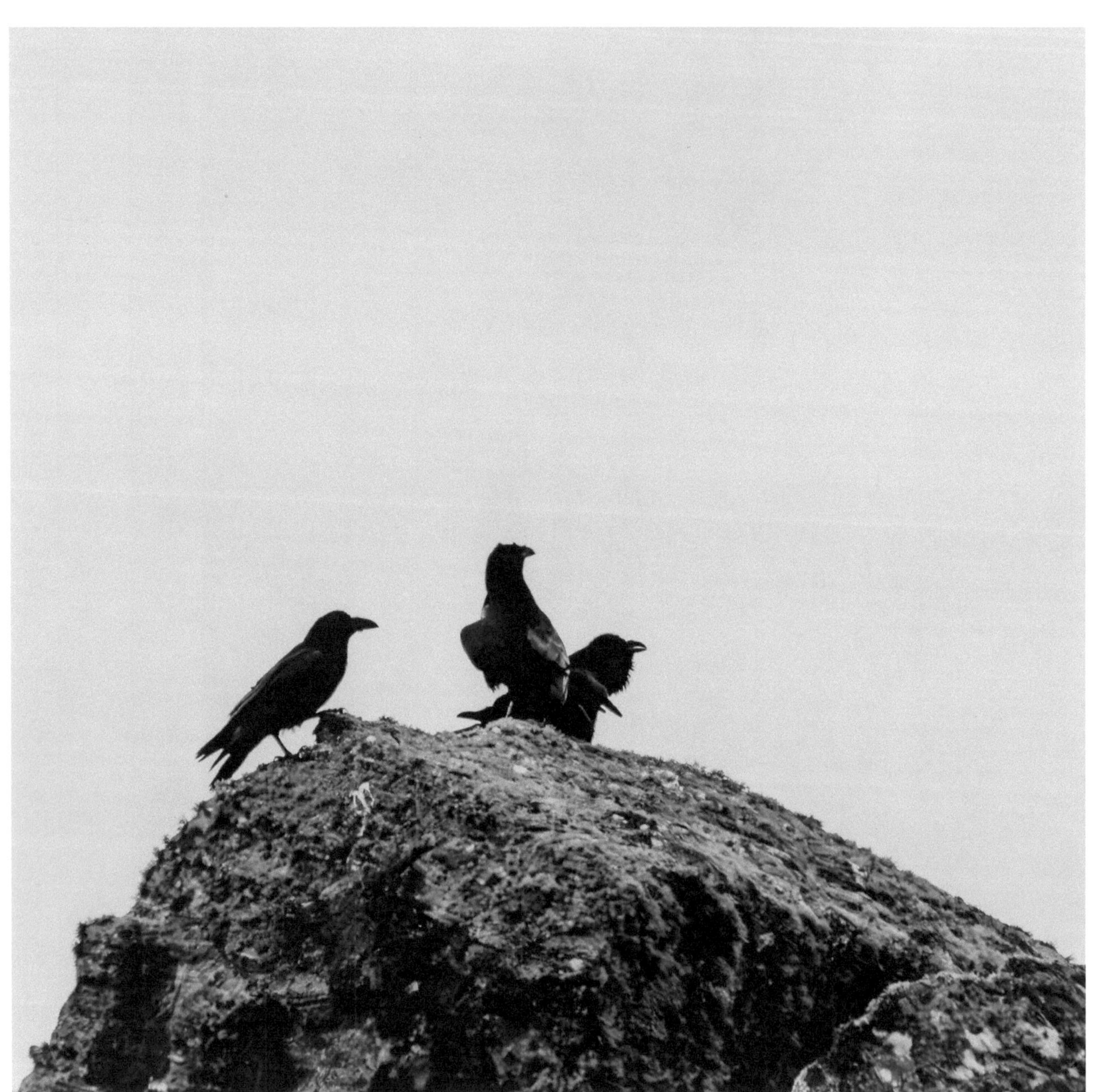

II

Sitting cross-legged on the altar stone
on the eve of Our Lady, Virgin and Queen.
The tide has closed behind me. Henbane's black
mantilla falls. My seat is a sooty pillar
of spindrift, set beneath the cross of the Lord,
under the gallows of Óðinn. Low waves ripple
on Doirlinn's strand, the echo of a lay from Bòrnais—
Herthjof held the victory in the Hebrides against us;
Rogvald met his ruin before the rain of shields.
Doubtless the battle-gulls waded in blood,
as at Øresund, Waterford, York. They smote
with their swords, then hammered them to ploughshares:
a few acres of barley, some cows and sheep,
maybe a chug-a-lug crab boat—*boireannach, feuch do mhac!*
Malefactors feast in the Christian Valhǫll,
according to Grimkill, Bishop of Trondheim.
Also at their father's table, the tables of their sons;
which every oppressor calls justice, and every man
of war calls peace. I fell from the altar, and rolled
in sopping grass. Eels wriggled up my trouser-legs,
the sleeves of my plastered shirt. They fastened
in my house of flesh and sucked me like leeches.
Their bite was sharp, their slime was cold,
their icthyotoxins sweet. At that point I seemed
to begin this song. I came to at dawn,
when the ravens returned and the sea started chucking its buckets:
this thing with empty sockets, ringed in living blood.
I waded to shore, cradling my waxy carcase.

III

By the last week in May, the young are aloft
and the nest is vacant. They hang around
the stones all summer, the unroofed vaults
of the burial ground. Always three, except this year,
when the parents somehow managed six:
the picked-apart ewe, washed-up below the eyrie,
a possible explanation. Or driven off the crag
like a mammoth. Body parts scattered
above the cove suggest the staple diet is rabbit.
The desiccate bristles of an unzipped hedgehog;
a snakebird's splay-winged shock of corpse;
pilfered hen's eggs, a swan's from the pile
on Loch a' Brugha—the laboured commute
over Smeircleit to West Kilbride—gibbetted
hoodies, the tombs of Ceann a' Ghàraidh.
They fly to and fro and miss nothing,
neither wolf, nor bear, or white-tailed eagle,
the upright butchers of the long cloud's long white strand.
Did they cronk across the Sound to their kin
on high Sciathan, *Come feast on the dolphin's bounty*?
A dozen erupted from Böðvar's tide-dumped corpse—
What is this sleep that holds you now?
You are lost in the dark and cannot hear me.
The price is always the death of children.
Poetry is never any consolation, whether stammered
by the meek at sandy gravesides, or declaimed
in cathedrals by the elocute knaves of the mighty.
It wheedles like Grima and crows like the Daily Mail.
Only the raven can sing the raven's lay.
He watched them tumble over Skallagrim's mound,
cronk or eighty different calls, the runes
of their sibylline aerobatics. They fly to and fro
over rising waters, and every year, return.

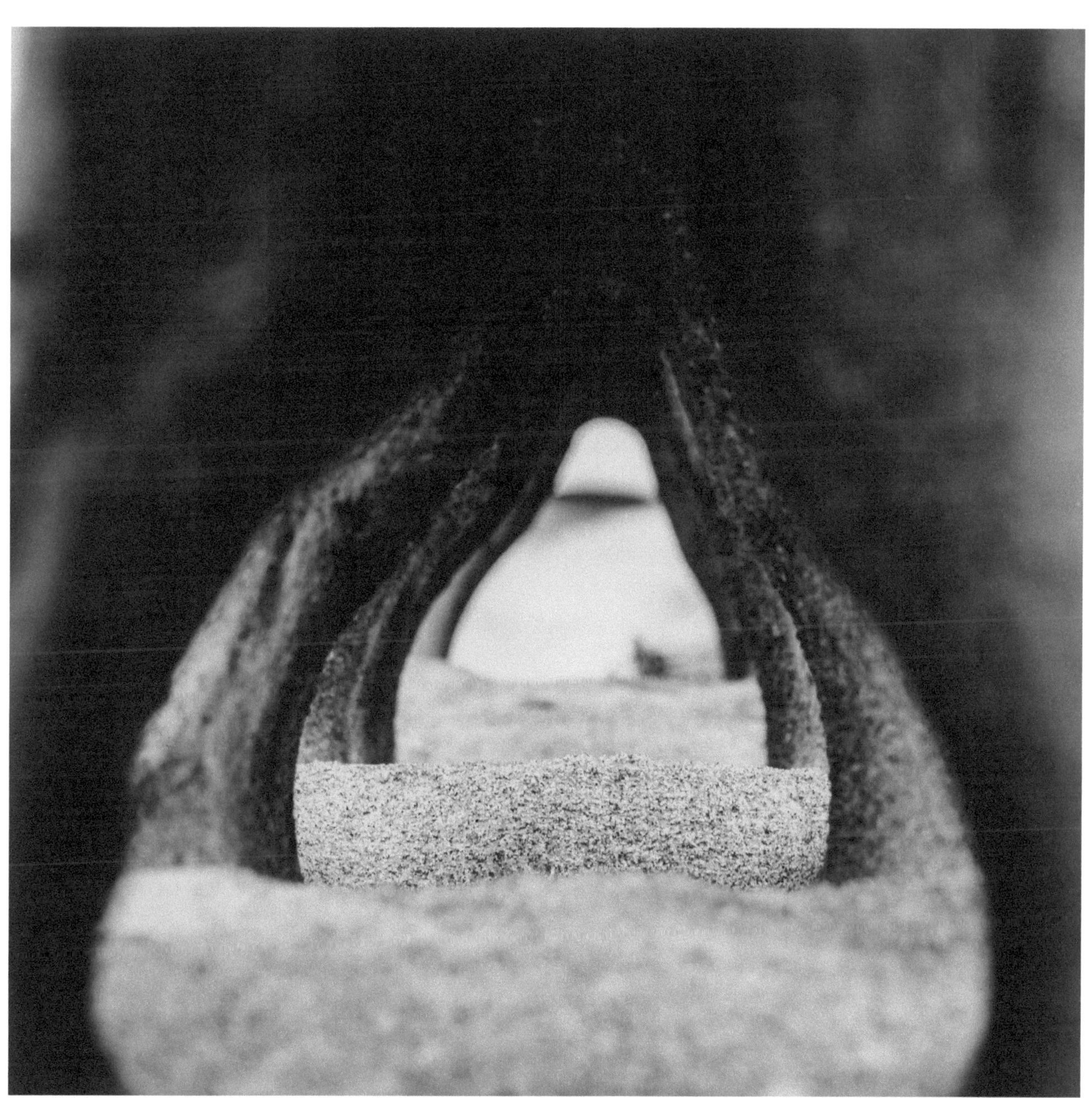

THE BURIAL GROUND

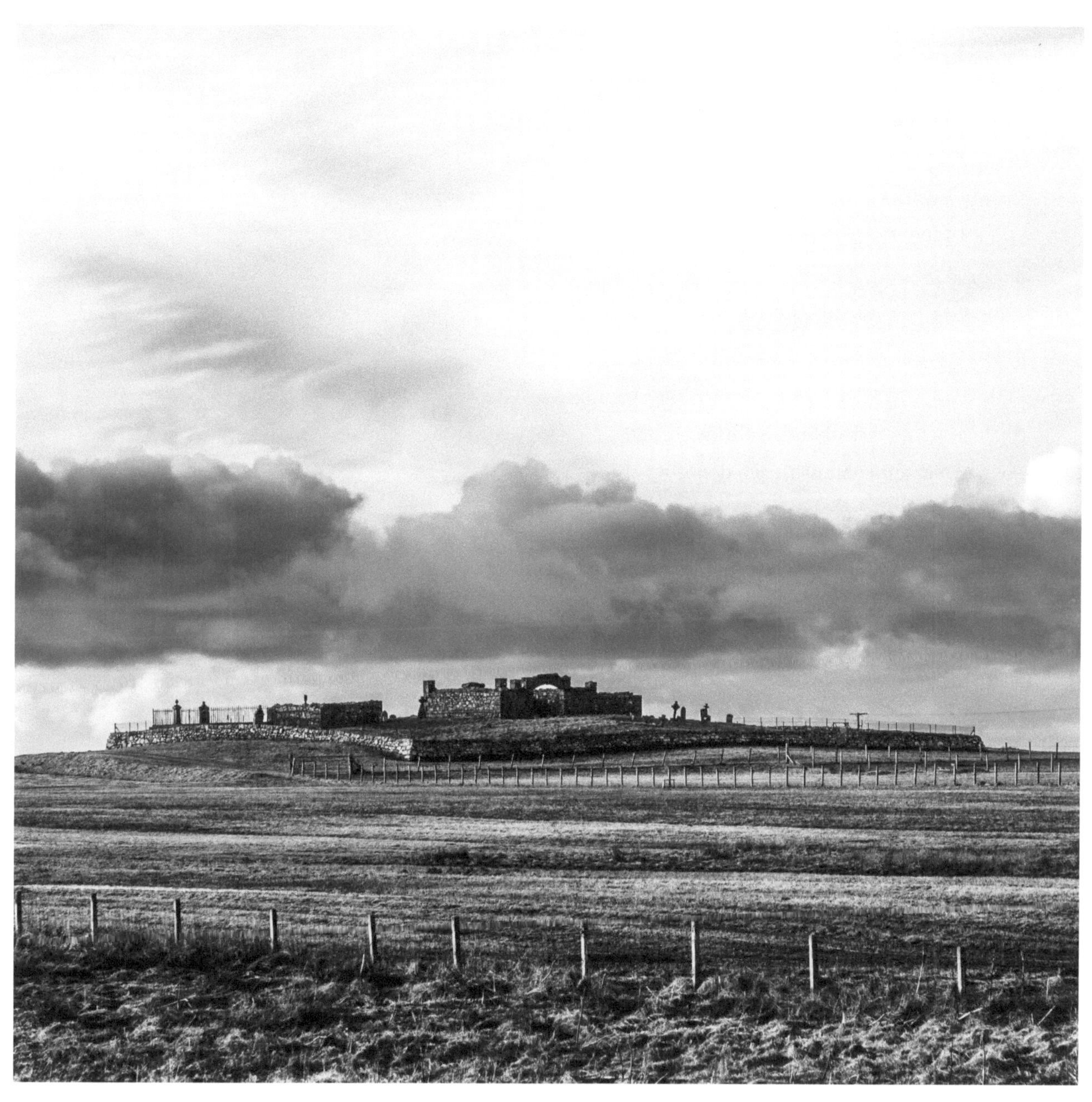

Every man should be a farmer and till his own land.
His croft might be small—a few acres of barley,
a couple of goats and a stone house thatched with reeds—
but it's all he needs to fill his belly and keep him living free.
— Hávamál, 36-37.

I

Bÿisdaill on the machair in the windbreak
shadow of *Soa*. A little Dutch city
in careful perspective, towers & spires, etc.
Joan Blaeu, 1654, based on Timothy Pont,
around 1600. *Bûyſdale*. No chapel, church
or burial ground, though *Kilphedre* has its cross.
Cille Pheadair, the cell of Peter, St. Peter's kirk,
or kirkyard. *Boisdale* on the machair
in the windbreak shadow of *Ornsay* Island,
the bled white tack of high Kilbride.
Fourteen careful oblongs, each denoting
a house or building. No chapel, church
or burial ground. William Bald, 1805.
The burial ground on the Baghasdail machair,
just south of Bald's obliterated village.
In Orasaigh's shadow, a few hundred yards
north-east of Sgeir na Cille. Explorer 453.

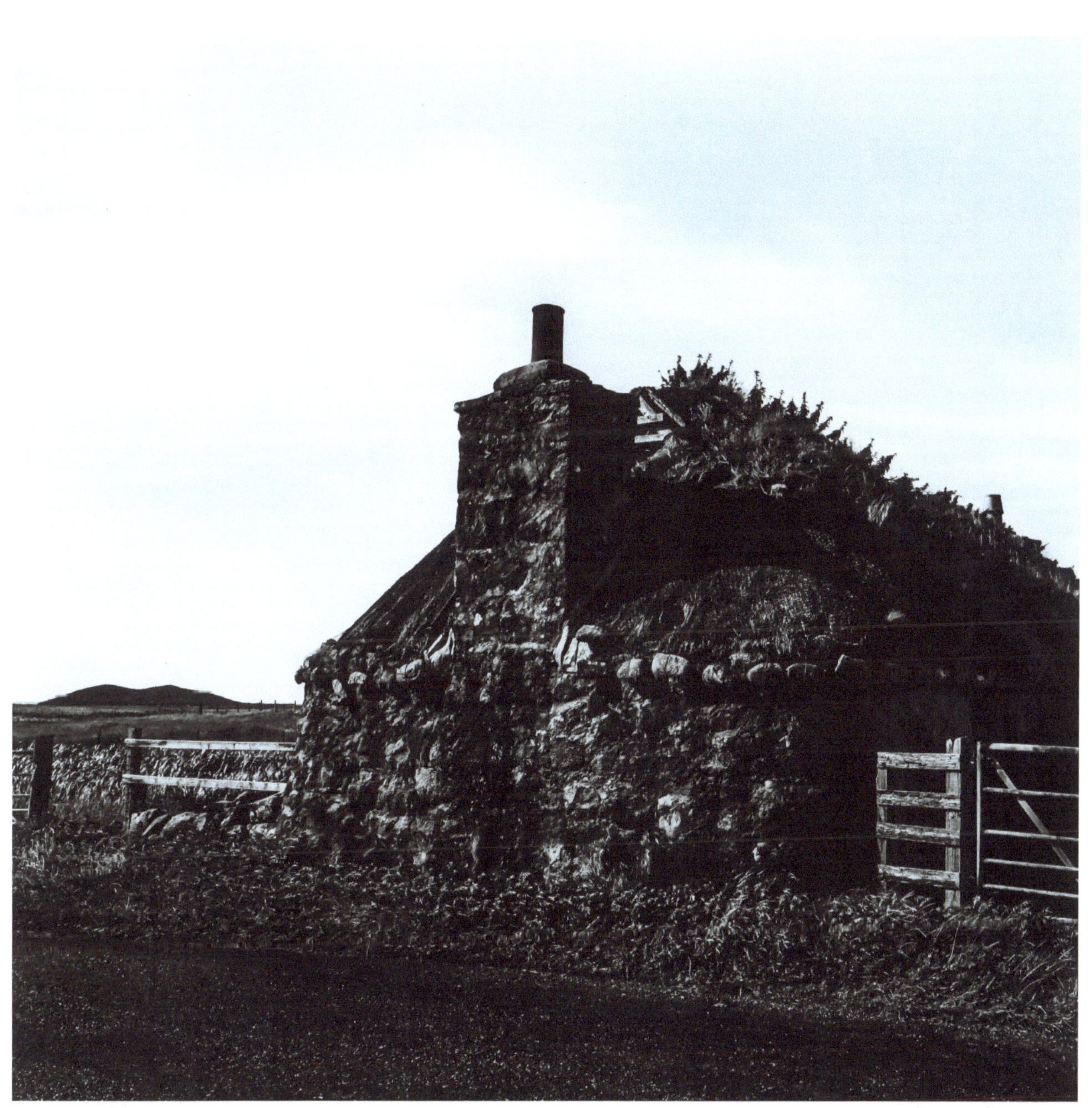

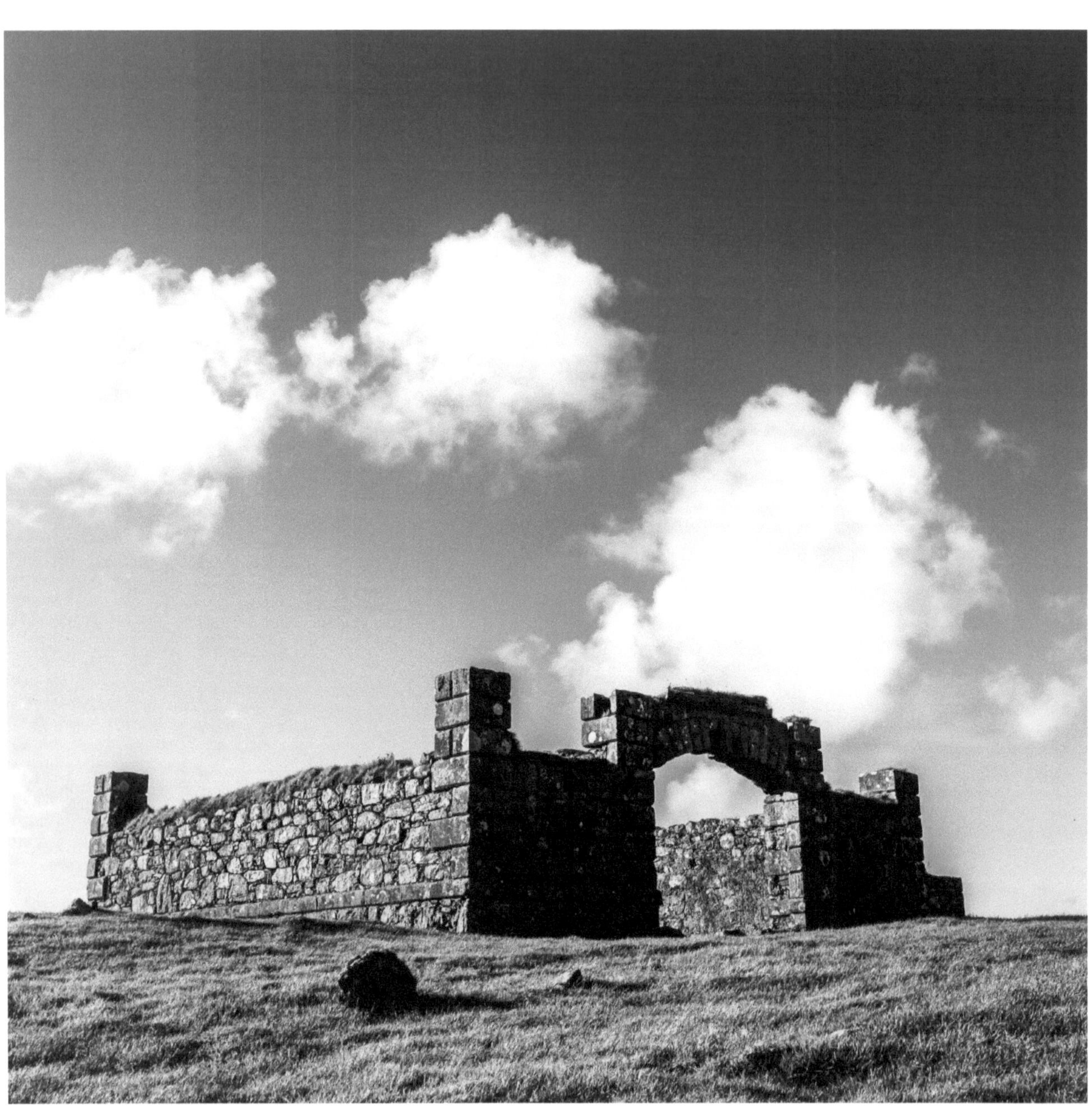

II

A wonky, walled-off acre, enclosing
an ancient settlement mound, its ten-metre contour
of stratified dead. 'Supposed site of a chapel',
where the Great Bull of Boisdale
seceded from the faith of Rome and joined
the cult of Mammon. Four dilapidated vaults,
a scatter of leaning stones, some fallen;
plenty more sunk beneath the trampoline sod.
The three-foot, drystone wall is topped
with a grey steel, chain-link fence, to protect
the dead from the blasphemies of sheep.
Or cage their vengeful ghosts. Rabbits collapse
the lichened walls and starlings hurtle in-and-out
of gaps between the stones; once a lapwing
trailed its wing across the mounded graves.
Generally ravens, leaping the arch of the gap-toothed vault
that yawns from the graveyard's summit.
The metal gate says close the gate
and Commonwealth War Grave.
Someone comes down with a strimmer.

III

The Great Bull is somewhere under this turf.
Wynne drove the Little Bull out. He's under the sod
at Greyfriars, where no dog waits but to worry
his bones. Three from the Merchant Navy,
one a nameless, flotsam stranger. A major
of the Gordon 6th, under the turf at Anzio,
listed with his brothers on his parents' modest stone.
MacLellans, MacKenzies, Pattersons and Stewarts;
every second stone a Ferguson, even beyond
the spike-fenced walls of their privy family vault.
Little pharaohs of the machair, piling their pyramids,
gibbeting their lapwings. Sand and time have devoured
the Israelites' unmarked graves. Their monument
is their own survival, their remembrance, their tongue.

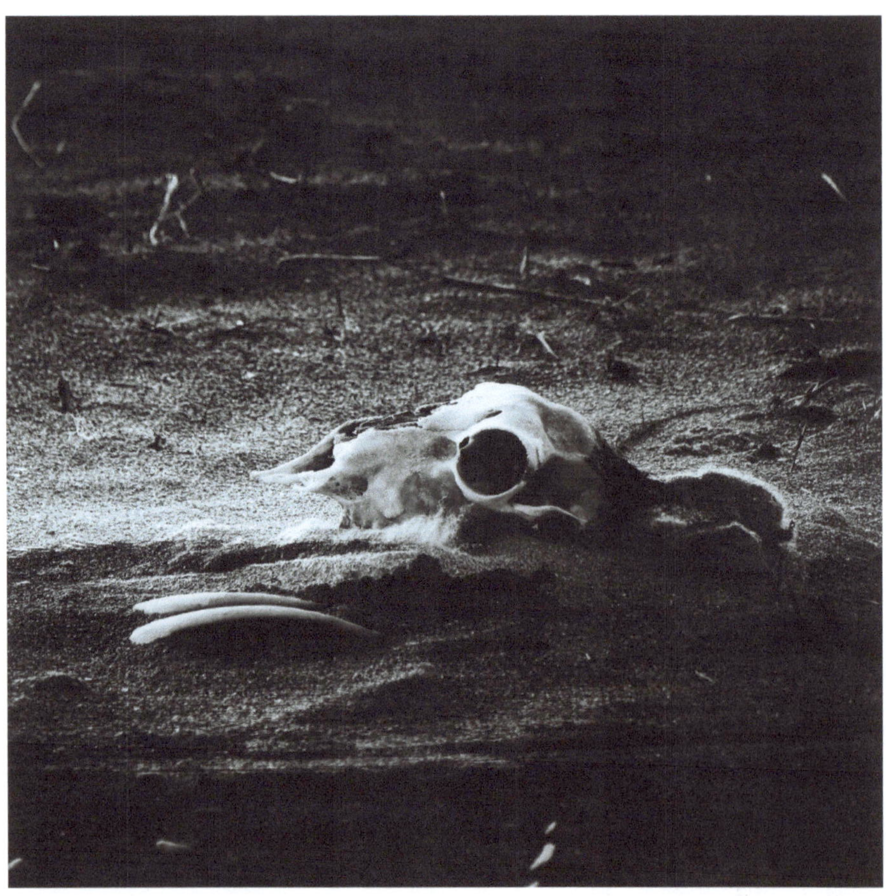

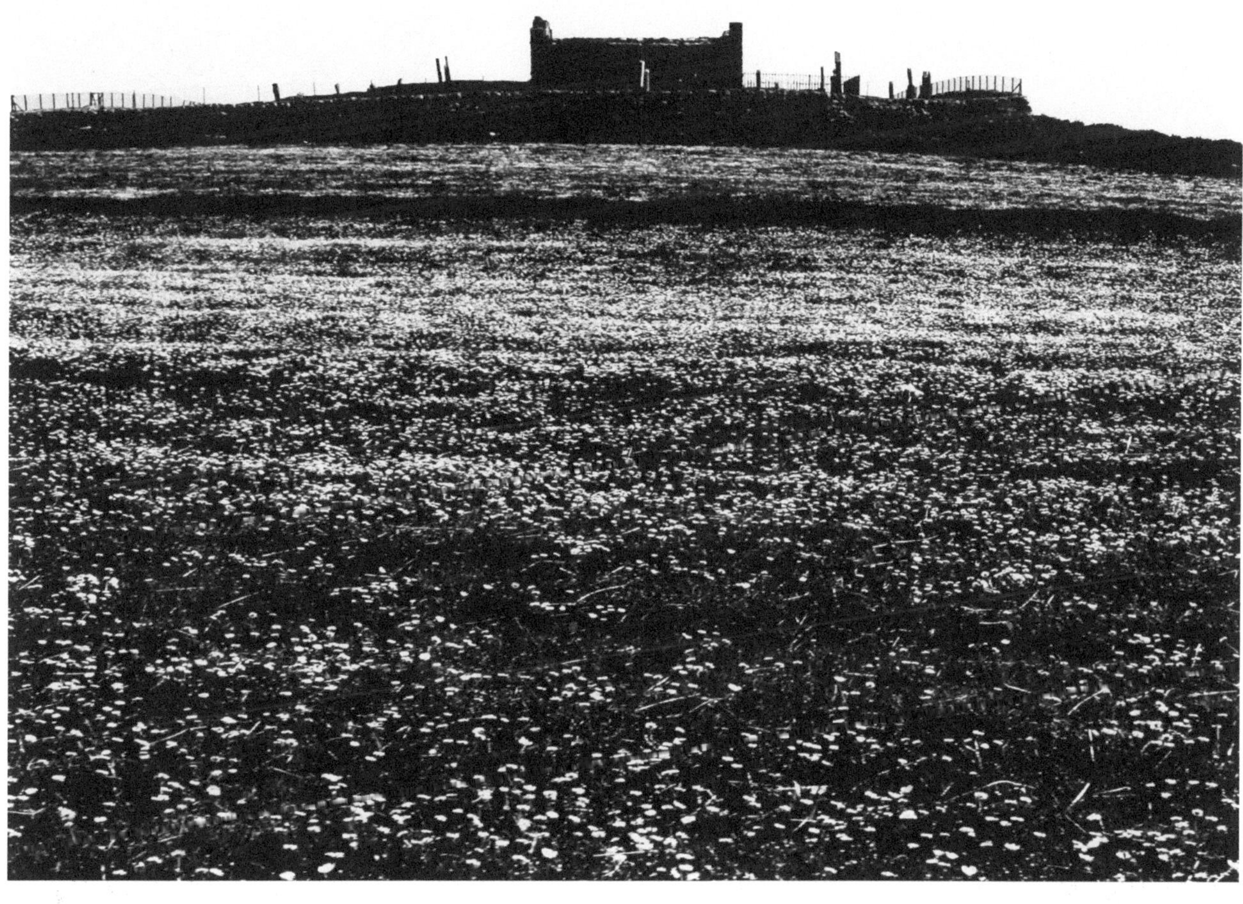

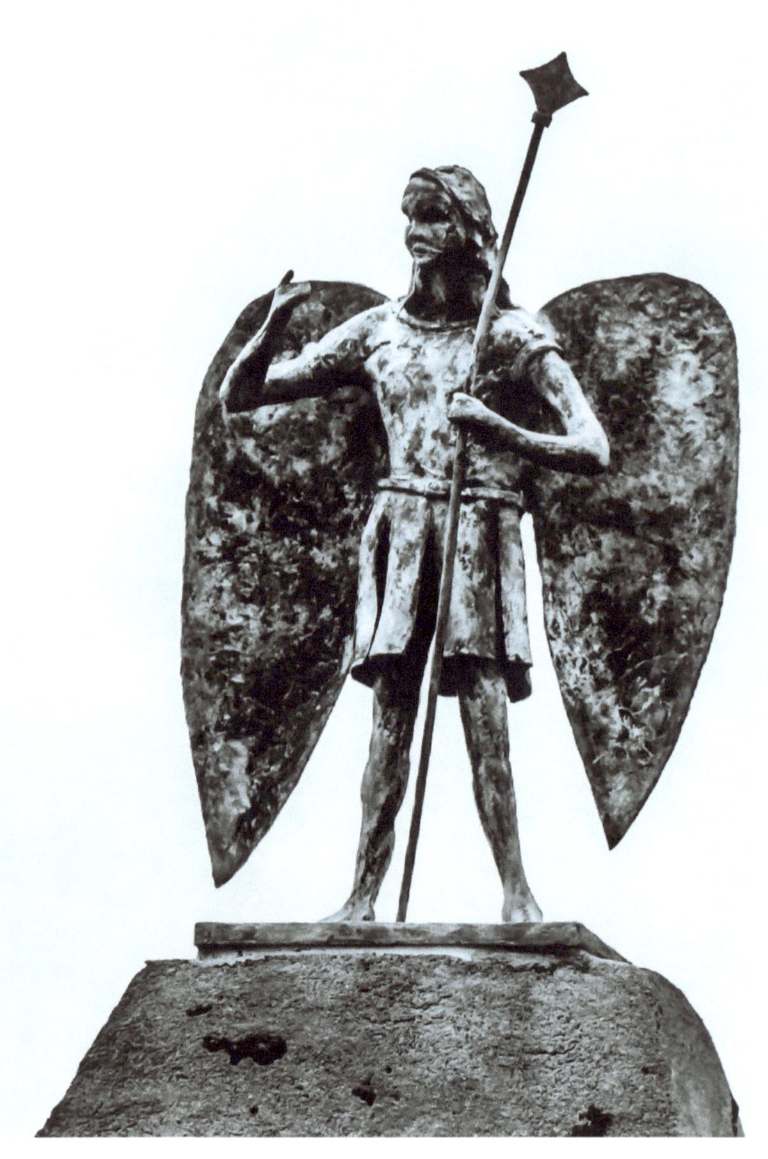

IV

The trouble with Papists (1). Too many Feasts
and Saint's Days. Keeps them from the kelp.
The trouble with Papists (2). Their little plots
and lazybeds. Keeps them from the kelp.
The trouble with Papists (3). They speak the Papist tongue.
Keeps them from the Presbyterian pulpit.
Keeps them from the Presbyterian Word.
Keeps them from the Presbyterian kelp.
The trouble with Papists (4). They refuse to starve
that I might toss another sack of sovereigns
on the pile. With my yellow rod, I would
drive them to Geneva. With my yellow rod,
I would raise weals across their shoulders.
With my yellow rod, I would ram mutton
down the throats of their fasting children.
With my factor, bailiffs and solicitors,
I would quadruple their rents and give
their daughters to the Elders. Also their sons.
They are not permitted dogs. The trouble
with Papists (5). They withdraw their labour
and defy their Master, his factor, bailiffs,
solicitors. Provokes in their Master apoplexy.
Keeps them from the kelp. The trouble with Papists (6).
They emigrate to Prince Edward Island.
Keeps them from the kelp. The trouble with Papists (7).
Being damned they confound God's Elect.
Keeps me awake at night. Keeps me from adding
to 'my considerable patrimony'. Keeps me from the kelp.

V

The Hunkpapa Sioux, starved to surrender
on the slopes of White Mountain, Saskatchewan.
Sitting Bull's ghost in his tartan ghost shirt
drinking whisky out of a paper bag
on a bench at the Regina Highland Games—
beaten through the heather, driven up the gangplanks,
tossed bound upon the decks. Eating grass
with the jaws of sheep from Nova Scotia
to Vancouver Island. Red sky at morning,
shepherd's warning—low roofs of flaming reeds.
Beaten from their villages, driven up the gangplanks,
chained below the decks: a special delivery
for John Gordon of Cluny, M.P. for Weymouth
and Melcombe Regis, the gate of the Black Death—
fifteen-hundred 'negro' slaves for his plantations
in Tobago. Twenty-five grand in reparations,
1833. Ranald *George* MacDonald,
seventy-three grand in champagne debt,
racking his starving tenants. Dancing a reel
at his King's command: the basilisk cult
of Old Etonian sporran. *O, for the Bonnie Prince's broadsword!*
Three thousand 'white negroes', dumped
into Sitting Bull's west. The Great Mother
had no reservations. This earth is strange
and these bones are not my own. MacMhuirich's ghost
in his tartan ghost shirt, sipping uisge-beatha
from Wovoka's skull at the Braemar Highland Games.

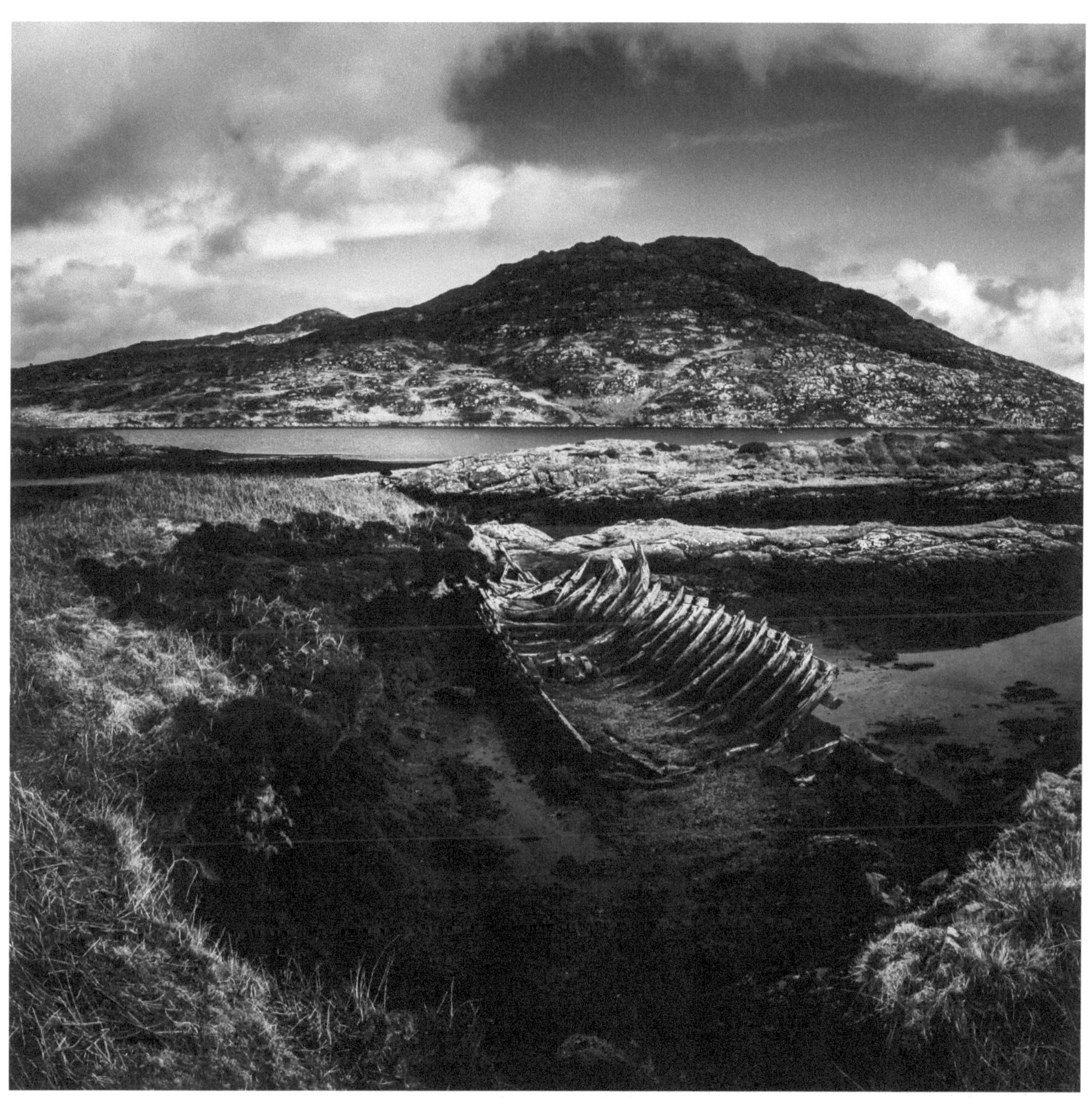

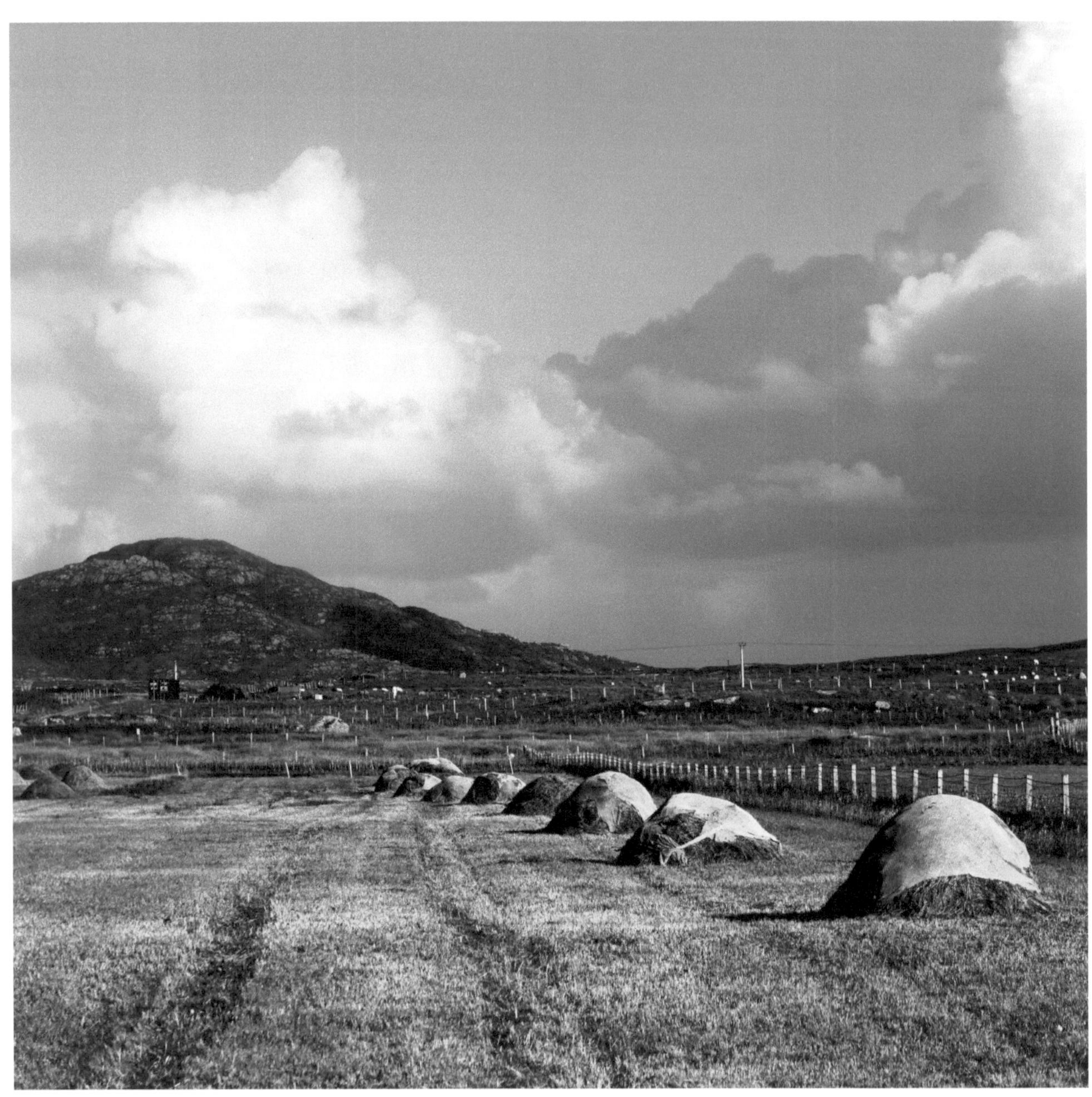

VI

Light Shining in Inverness-shire;
the fences broken and locked sod turned
at Calbhaigh and Bhatarsaigh, Nuntonhill.
Let pharaohs rage and their factors plot vain things,
for we have sown parsnips, carrots and beans,
in this earth, our common treasury.
No man will Lord or command his own kind,
nor shall we creep up one another's arses
for honours. Throw down their silver Hartichoaks,
their just-asses of the Peace! MacMhuirich established
his Soviet on the machair, with Connolly,
Cornford, Dimitrov, Stalin. In a dream
he called it Stòras Uibhist. Every man a farmer,
tilling his own land. Sharks lurking offshore:
the blitzkrieg capital of Emily Cathcart Gordon,
Trump or Wang Jianlin. The money-washing
percentage men of Turks & Caicos, City and Man.
And all the little pharaohs, their graft and crude
ambition, their bailiffs and solicitors—maggots
in the mutton, caterpillars in the cabbages.
They live on our labours, and give us bran to eat.

VII

Ravens cronk from the burial ground,
over the shell-holed machair. Hysterical
lapwings and oystercatchers harry them
on their way. Wind whips away the clamour,
the hush and whump of ocean. A little red tractor
raises its front-bucket horns like a beetle
and trundles its trailer down onto the beach
at the dune break to An Doirlinn. The ravens
give it a wide berth, climbing the wind
over Orasaigh Bagh until their flags unfurl
on the summits of the island. I rally to the banners.
Corncrakes crexing from the eight-inch grass
fall silent at my footsteps: they slink invisible
through the bent and resume their duel behind me.
Subsidy keeps them from shredding by combines,
and tourism chips in its quota—car stickers
proclaiming *I Slept With Corncrakes*, twittered
encounters with white-tailed eagles on the slope
below Beinn Mhòr. Raised fingers at every passing place.
The café and gift shop at the Kildonan Museum.
Yesterday's paper at Dalabrog Co-op.
Otter loping up the beach; turning, loping back.
The whippet doesn't know what it is.
Wreck of rotting kelp, front-bucketed
into the dripping trailer with a brace
of stiff gannets, flotsam from distant Sula,
where Lewismen club garefowl and harpoon
northern right whales. Drum-beats sound
in Orasaigh's forest and tall flames leap
on the western strand, where tonnage of sea cows
and bullock aurochsen drip from spits

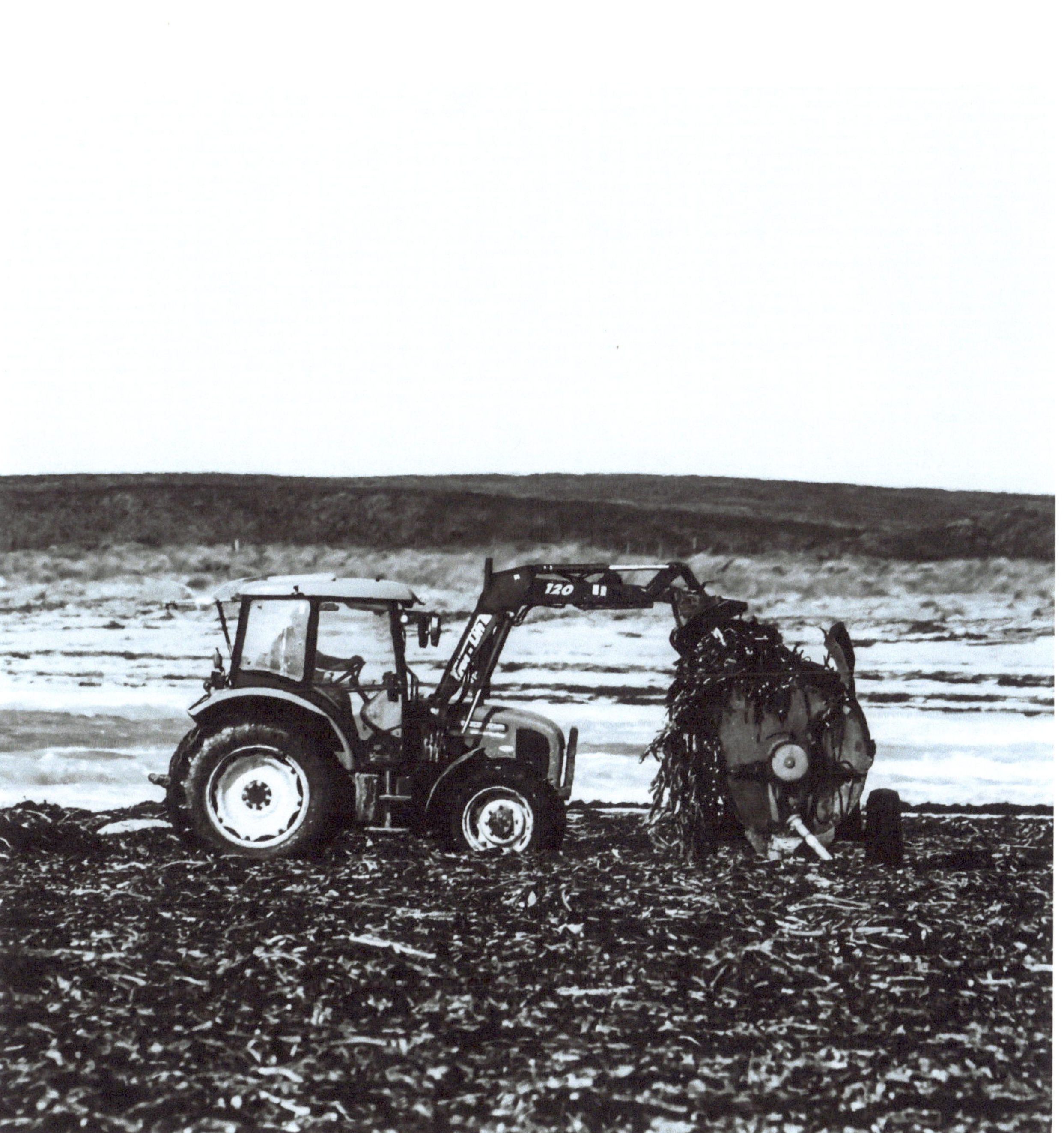
120

before the fire-glow's gilded thrones: chainsaws
of Gilgamesh, mace-heads of Scorpion II.
A family of ravens pick over their bones
on the beach. *'A shrewd businessman and as able*
a bowman as any in Scotland [...] a man of outstanding
abilities and active business habits [...] educated
at Eton [...] an assiduous, innovative and generous
landlord [...] has taken a very active
part in the management of her enormous estates
and has figured prominently
in connection with the crofter problem.'
[Hitler loved his dog, and figured prominently
in connection with the Jewish problem.]
The Great Mother let rip in the Empire
of Boisdale, all over her tickled pink world—
land as capital's lebensraum, enslavement as policy,
extinction as carnival, collateral damage.
The pink-headed duck and great Indian rhino,
the pot-bellied children of Skibbereen and Bengal.
Bagpipes, kilts, sgian-dubh. Old Tom Morris,
the weaver's lad. Hauled himself up
by his sillybod bootstraps to build a links
for the Lady on the cleared out Askernish machair.
Trump swinging his irons like Custer's sabre.
Trump signing his treaties with the repeating rifles
of the Seventh Cavalry. Spotted Elk frozen
like a gannet on the beach, hecatombs of buffalo,
burnt on the Wall Street machair. Bolsonaro,
Orban, Johnson. Cameron, Brown and Blair.
Horrible children, ripping the heads off Spix's macaws
at the Harewood Lane allotments. Parliament
ripping out their grown-up hearts with Amazon

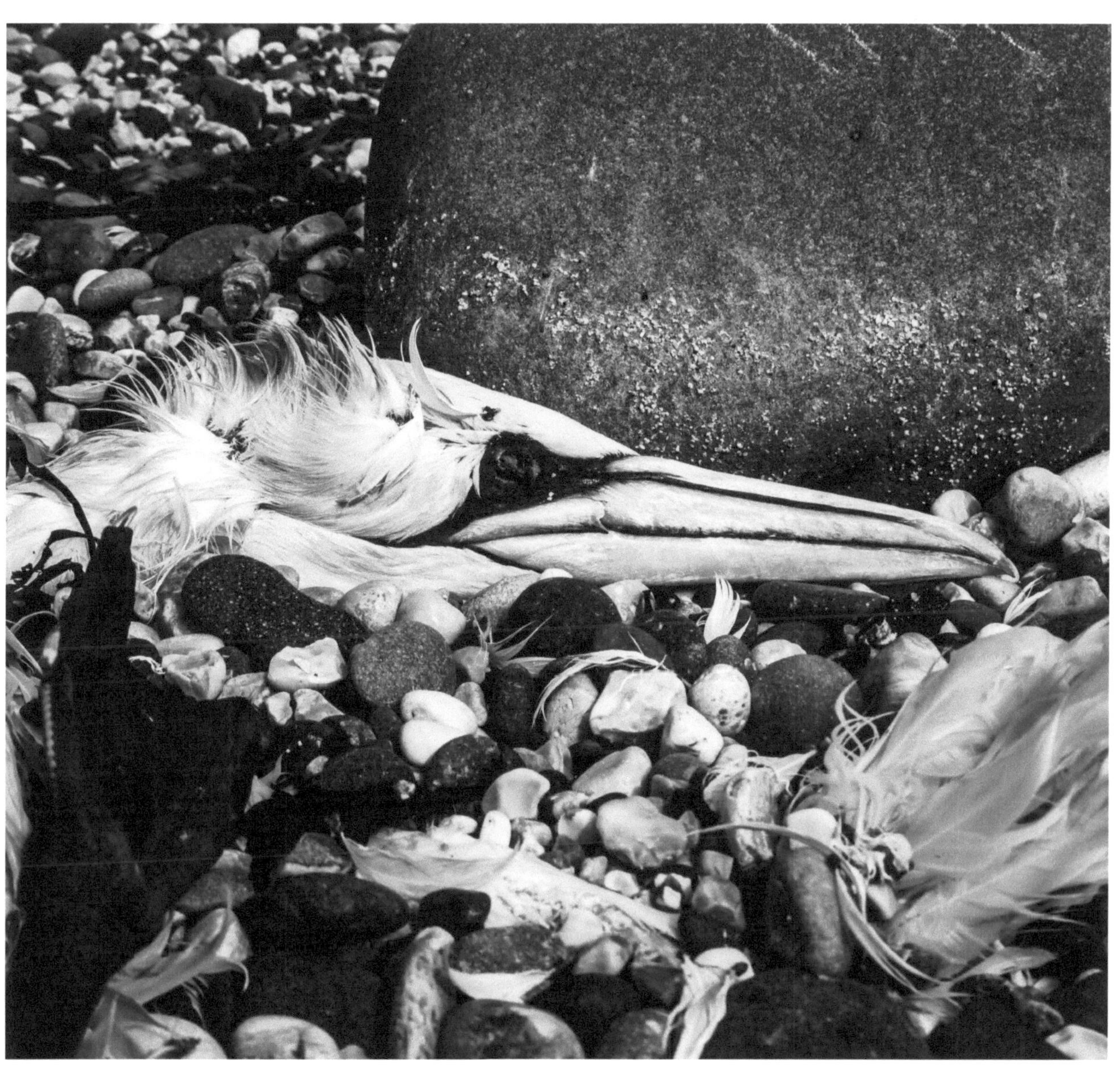

and HS2, for which they are truly grateful.
Reid and McGahey, Jeremy Corbyn,
donning their ghost shirts, bawled down
by the brexiting helots of England:
the working class, a weapon deployed against itself
by those who have enslaved them. Love Island
versus Poles and Pakis. Love Island versus
Greta Thunberg. Love Island versus doodlebugs
and Messerschmitt 109s—eight ravens over Orasaigh;
below An Doirlinn, a single black-backed gull.
Low tide laps and swells around the island,
a mile or two higher than it was five thousand years ago.
It will open the graves of the burial ground
and scatter the bones in the North Atlantic Drift.
A motorhome drops beneath the dunes;
ravens vaporise in the flare of the evening sun;
the black-backed gull has vanished. Cyclonic thunderheads
bleed their inks on the crab boat's west horizon.
The follicles of the cotton grass are rising.
Five thousand years of immaterial culture,
life on the literal edge—Hebrides, falling slowly.

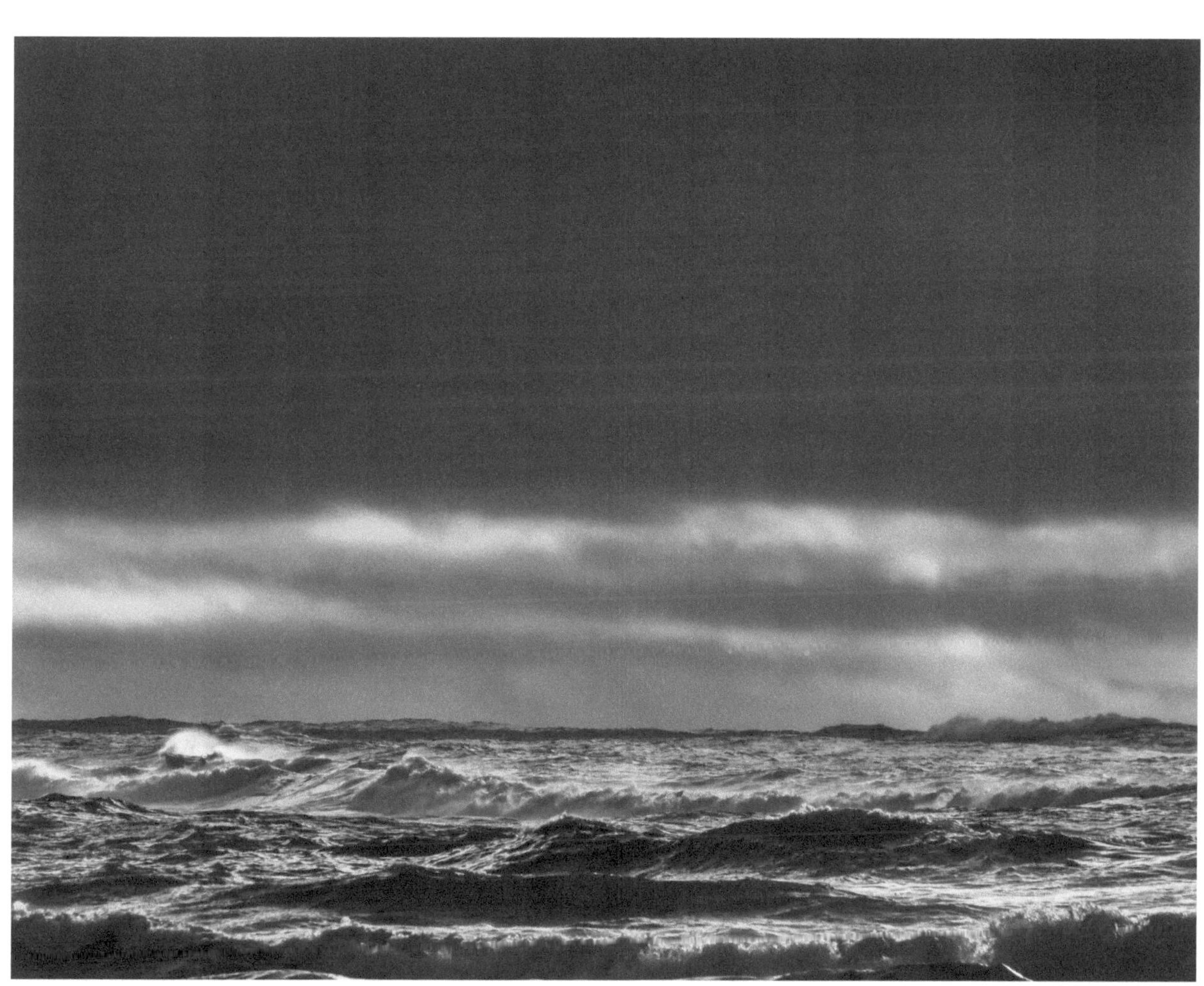

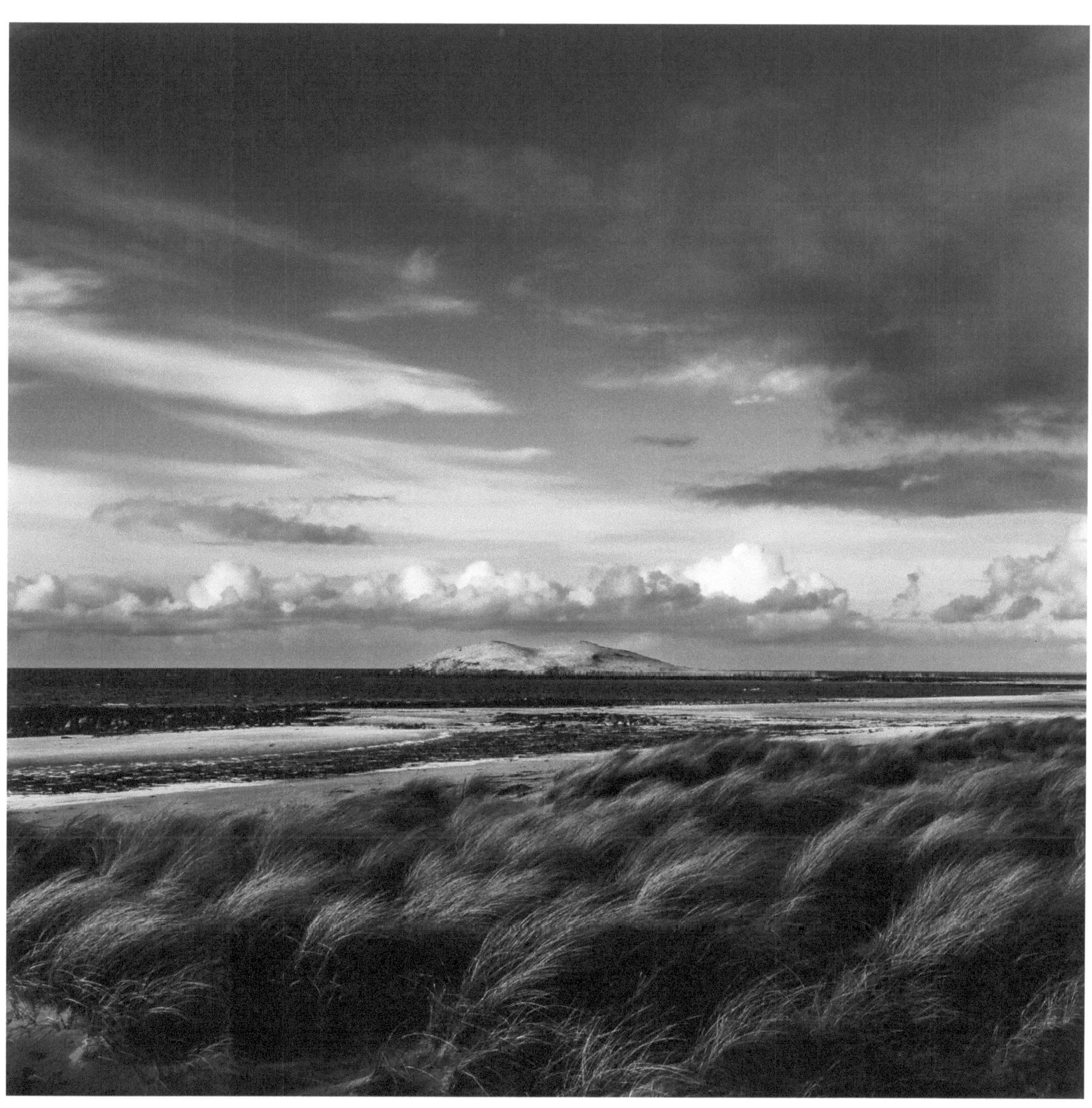

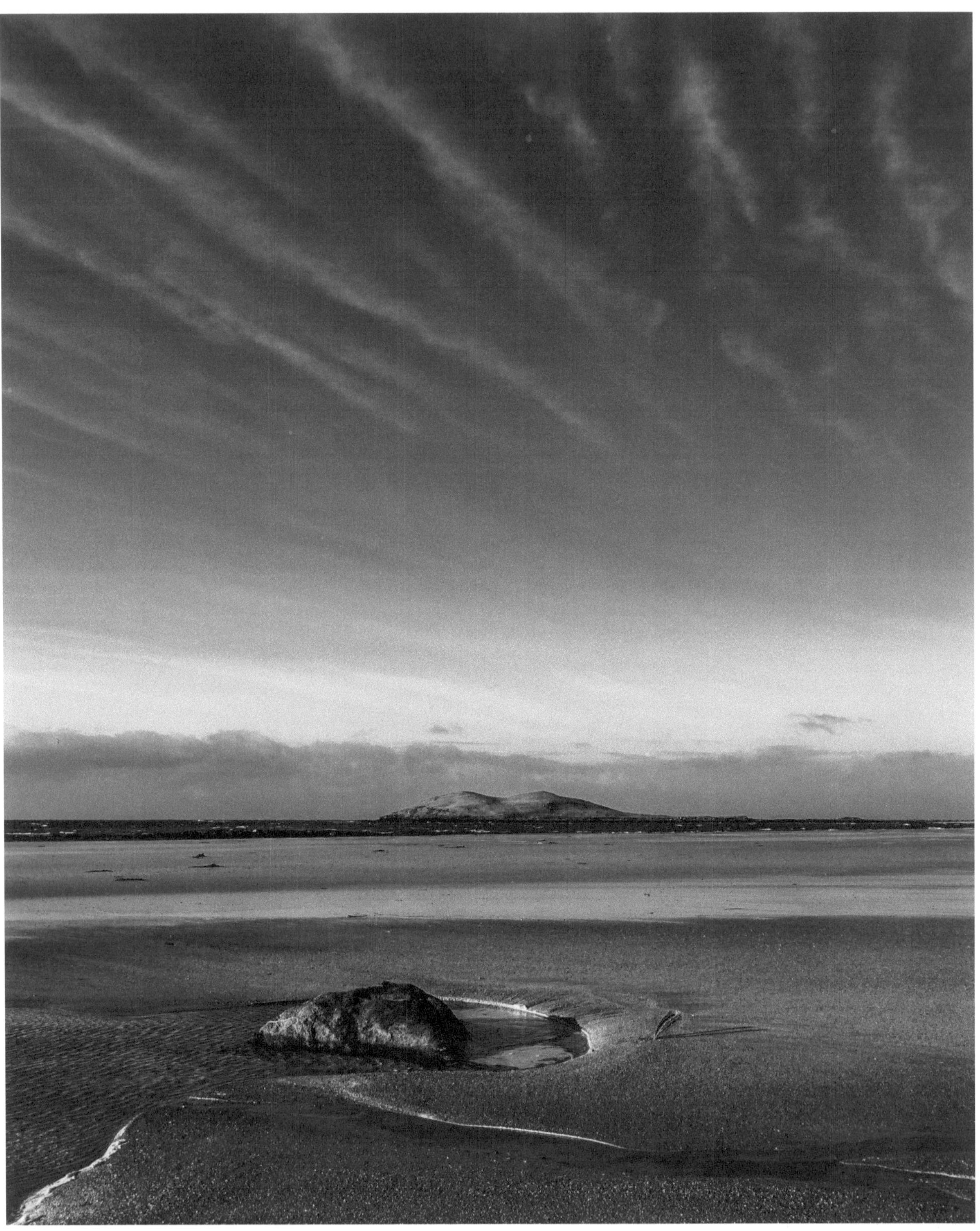

NOTES ON THE POEMS

Orasaigh: the 'faded road' was once the main highway of South Uist but is now little more than a track; 'lazybeds' or *feannagan* are the traditional, spade-turned, ridge-and-furrow plots of the Western Isles; 'eight-inch grass'—corncrakes move from the iris beds of the blackland on to the machair when the grass is about eight inches tall; 'Saglek Bay' is in North Labrador.

An Doirlinn: 'snekkja, bìrlinn, sgoth'—types of clinker-built boat used at various times in the Western Isles; 'Scorpion II' was a First Dynasty Egyptian king who reigned around 3000 BC, just before the historical 'Gilgamesh' began his reign in Sumer; humans extirpated 'sea cows' and 'garefowl' in the 18th and 19th centuries respectively; the italic lines beginning 'seven days and nights' are appropriated from *The Epic of Gilgamesh*; 'Aqualung' is an album by Jethro Tull, much loved by archaeology students; the 'serpopard' is one of the many species of animal that Gilgamesh boasted he had slaughtered; 'skraelings'—the name Leif Erikson gave to the people he encountered in Vinland, thought to be Native Americans; 'Spey Royal' was one of the brands of whisky liberated from the *S.S. Politician* by enterprising locals after the ship grounded off Eriskay in 1941; the five lines beginning 'A naked lady' and ending with 'lozenge of sand' reference the wreck of the emigrant ship the *Annie Jane* off Vatersay on 9th September 1853. Over 350 people were drowned and most were buried in mass graves in the dunes above Tràigh Siar. Many of the dead and survivors were robbed of their jewellery and clothing by locals; the italic lines beginning '*hunc tumulum ...*' are from the Catholic Benediction of the Grave; 'he' refers to John Gordon of Cluny (1776-1858), the absentee landlord who, in 1851, brutally evicted 3000 of his tenants from their homes in Barra, Eriskay, South Uist & Benbecula, and forcibly shipped them to Canada; 'mace [...] lapwings'—the Scorpion Macehead was excavated at Nekhen in 1899. The lapwings depicted as gibbeted on the macehead were symbols of the 'common folk' in the Egyptian iconography of the time.

The Stones: 'hvalsbak'—whale's back (Icelandic); 'ramalina' is the generic Latin name of sea ivory; 'Mike Parker Pearson' (b. 1957) is Professor of Later British History at the Institute of Archaeology, London. He has conducted extensive research in South Uist; 'Baldrick' refers to Tony Robinson (b. 1946) presenter of the TV show, *Time Team*; *The Modern Antiquarian* is the musician Julian Cope's (b. 1957) gazetteer of British megalithic sites; 'droch shùil' is the evil eye; 'Niall Sharples' (b. 1956) is Professor of Archaeology at Cardiff University and has researched extensively in South Uist, including excavations and surveys at Orasaigh and An Doirlinn. 'Neil Oliver' (b. 1967) is an archaeologist and broadcaster well-known as the presenter of TV shows such as *Vikings* and *Britain's Ancient Capital: Secrets of Orkney*. 'Terry Nutkins' (1946-2012) left home at the age of twelve to live and work with Gavin Maxwell (1914-1969) at Sandaig, the latter's Highland retreat, where one of Maxwell's pet otters bit off two of his fingers. Nutkins later became a children's TV presenter, working with Johnny Morris (1916-1999) on *Animal Magic*, and with Chris Packham (b. 1961) and Michaela Strachan

(b. 1966) on the *Really Wild Show.* The poet 'Kath Raine' (1908-2003) was besotted with Maxwell, despite her awareness of his homosexuality. John Aspinall (1926-2000) was the owner of a private zoo at which he'd feed his pet tigers with their keepers; 'Mubarak bin London' was the name allegedly given to Maxwell's friend Wilfrid Thesiger (1910-2003) by the Marsh Arabs of Iraq. Aspinall's crony Lord 'Lucan' is missing, as the Dodgems repeatedly pointed out. The 'Baronets of Nova Scotia' were Scotsmen enobled by successive Stuart monarchs in return for commitments to plant settlers in Nova Scotia. They did so by making living conditions for their Scottish tenants so unendurable that emigration seemed preferable to remaining on their ancestral plots, later adding indenture, the press gang and forcible eviction to their repertoire of methods for planting their sovereign's New World. The lines from 'Hallaig' to 'Leipzig' reference the poetry of the communist poet Somhairle MacGill-Eain (Sorley MacLean, 1911-1996), whose poetry praised the Irish-Scottish socialist James 'Connolly' (1968-1916), the Bulgarian revolutionary 'Georgi Dimitrov' (1882-1949) and the communist poet John 'Cornford' (1915-1936), who fought with the International Brigades and was killed in the Spanish Civil War; Mick McGahey (1925-1999) was a Scottish miner, a member of Communist Party of Great Britain (CPGB) and ultimately vice-President of the National Union of Mineworkers; 'a rat race is for rats' is a phrase from the famous speech given by Jimmy Reid (1932-2010) on the occasion of his election to the role of Rector of Glasgow University in 1972. Reid was a communist and shop steward at Upper Clyde Shipbuilders and led the 'work-in' of 1971/72. In later life his political views changed and he left the CPGB for the Labour Party and latterly the Scottish Nationalists.

The Raven's Eyrie: the italic lines beginning 'Herthjof' are taken from Ragnarr Loðbrók's *Krákumál*, 'The Lay of the Raven'; *'boireannach, feuch do mhac!'*—'Woman, Behold your Son!' (John 19:26); 'Sciathan' is the highest hill on Eriskay; 'Böðvar' was Egil Skallagrimson's son. Egil's poem *Sonatorrek* expresses the grief he felt when Böðvar was drowned at sea and the consolation he found in poetry; the italic lines beginning '*What is this sleep*', are taken from Gilgamesh's lament for Enkidu in *The Epic of Gilgamesh*. 'Grima' is the wife of Áke in *The Saga of Ragnarr Loðbrók*; according to the *Handbook of the Birds of the World*, ravens have over 'eighty different calls', each with its specific purpose and utility.

The Burial Ground: Kilbride in South Uist was the seat of Alastair 'Mor nam Mart' MacDonald of Boisdale (1698-1768) and his descendants. Alastair's line initially held Boisdale as a tack from the clan chief MacDonald of Sleat, before being granted a feu charter to the property in 1758; 'Great Bull of Boisdale'—the aforementioned Alastair, a man renowned for his violence and physical prowess; the 'Little Bull' is his son Colin MacDonald (d. 1800); 'Wynne' is Matthias Wynne OP, the Dominican missionary who drove an apoplectic Colin MacDonald out of his church on 29th September, 1770, when the Little Bull disrupted the service in an attempt to force his Catholic tenants to work during the Feast of St. Michael. The cult of St. Michael seems to have been particularly strong in the southern Western Isles. As late as the early 20th century, locals referred to the saint as 'the god Michael', and regarded him as the patron of boats, horses and horsemen. On his feast day a special bannock (the

Struan Micheil) was made from all the different kinds of cereal grown on a given holding, baked in a lambskin and blessed at Mass by the priest. This was followed by horse races (both men and women participating, two to a horse, with women riding seated behind the men) and feasting; 'the jaws of sheep' is a phrase from a prophetic poem by Angus MacMhurich, who foresaw that the introduction of large scale sheep farming in the Western Isles would devour the land of the indigenous crofting population, lead to the breakdown of clan and kinship ties and ultimately the clearing of dependant clansmen from the land. The MacMhurichs were the hereditary bards of Clanranald (Clan MacDonald) before the post-1745 collapse of the clan system; Ranald George MacDonald (1788-1873) was the chief of Clanranald. He was Member of Parliament for the rotten borough of Plympton Erle, Devon, and the absentee landlord of large tracts of the Highlands and Western Isles, including South Uist. He neglected his estates and grievously exploited his impoverished tenants, seeing them only as a source of rent, which he would extract to the full even when his tenants were starving, using the monies gained to fund his extravagant lifestyle in the most exclusive circles of London society. Heavily indebted, he was forced to dispose of his estates in 1838, with the Barra to Benbecula stretch of his Hebridean holdings being sold to Lieutenant-Colonel John Gordon of Cluny Castle, Aberdeenshire; '*O for the Bonnie Prince's Broadsword*'—the Hanoverian monarch George IV was much taken by MacDonald's habit of wearing full Highland dress in London society (MacDonald played an important role in developing the Unionist royal family's ongoing infatuation with shortbread-tin Highland culture) and presented him with the Bonnie Prince's captured broadsword as a gift—knowing, of course, that such a man would never swing it in anger against the Hanoverian Crown; 'uisge-beatha'—whisky; 'Wovoka' (1865-1932)—the Paiute medicine man who inspired the second Ghost Dance movement in 1889/90; 'Light Shining in Inverness-Shire' references the anonymous Digger pamphlet of 1648, 'Light Shining in Buckinghamshire'. Lines and phrases from the pamphlet are embedded throughout section VI; Angus 'MacMhurich' is here conflated with Sorley MacLean, who translated MacMurich's 'jaws of sheep' poem, 'Lament for the Clearances', into English; 'Stòras Uibhist' is the community-owned company that purchased the South Uist estate in 2004 and manages the southern islands of Benbecula, South Uist and Eriskay; 'Emily Cathcart Gordon' (1848-1932) inherited the South Uist Estate from her husband John Gordon (son of the Lieutenant-Colonel) in 1878 and held it until her death in 1932. She managed the estate in the tradition of her father-in-law, racking and exploiting her tenants and encouraging 'emigration'; 'Wang Jianlin' (b. 1954) is the richest man in China; the long italic section in section VII comprises five 'found' descriptions of Alastair 'Mor nam Mart' MacDonald, Colin MacDonald, Ranald George MacDonald, Lieutenant-Colonel John Gordon and Emily Cathcart Gordon, respectively; the pink-headed duck and great Indian rhino were made extinct (the former) and brought to the brink of extinction (the latter) by the British during the period of the Raj; 'Spix's macaw' is a South American parrot, extinct in the wild due to the destruction of its habitat and the capture of wild birds for the pet trade.

NOTES ON THE PHOTOGRAPHS

The photographs in this book were made in direct response to the poem and produced specifically for this collaboration. The images are of the landscape and life of Uist, mainly South Uist, and the majority focus on the area around the island of Orasaigh.

ACKNOWLEDGEMENTS

Steve Ely would like to thank the following people who were involved in various ways in the development of *Orasaigh* - poem, book and wider project: the photographers Alex Boyd and Fiona MacIsaac, who were involved in the development of the concept in its early stages; Ed Reiss and Michael Stewart for their perceptive comments on an early draft of the poem, which led to several improvements; Andy MacKinnon, Arts Manager and UistFilm Director at Taigh Chearsabhagh, Lochmaddy, without whose vision, hard-work and support the two 2023 'Orasaigh' exhibitions at Cnoc Soilleir and at Taigh Chearsabhagh, and the range of workshops, talks, previews and launches associated with them, would simply not have been possible; Agnes MacDonald and the team at Cnoc Soilleir for hosting and facilitating the first exhibition; the composer Duncan MacLeod, for setting the poem to his hauntingly beautiful and evocative music in gallery and soundwalk settings; Juraj Fajnor of the University of Huddersfield for his recordings of the poem, and for making recordings in the Orasaigh landscape that Duncan was able to include in his compositions; Professor Hyunkook Lee of the University of Huddersfield for providing the cutting edge recording technology Juraj used in making the recordings; Alex O' Henley, who did his best to teach me how to pronounce the Gaelic words I incorporated into the poem; Roddy and Fiona MacInnes, in whose Boisdale holiday cottage I often stayed, with a direct line of sight to Orasaigh, only a few hundred yards distant; my mate Pat Mulhern, for his company on dozens of walks in the landscape, and for sharing my enthusiasm for Uist; and finally, to the people of Uist, those hard-working, resilient, resourceful, creative, good-humoured and hospitable custodians of their unique landscape, language, history and culture. *Tìr a' mhurain, tìr an eòrna, Tìr 's am pailt a h-uile seòrsa, Far am bi na gillean òga, Gabhail òran 's 'g òl an leanna.* Here's to another five-and-a-half thousand years on the edge of the world.

Michael Faint would like to thank the following: Steve Ely for the invitation to collaborate on a seemingly straightforward project; Alex Boyd for his recommendation to Steve; Simon Hart and Andy MacKinnon of Taigh Chearsabhagh for their support for the exhibitions; Hyunkook Lee, Juraj Fajnor and Duncan MacLeod for their work on the sound; most importantly to Sarah, without whom these pictures would not exist.

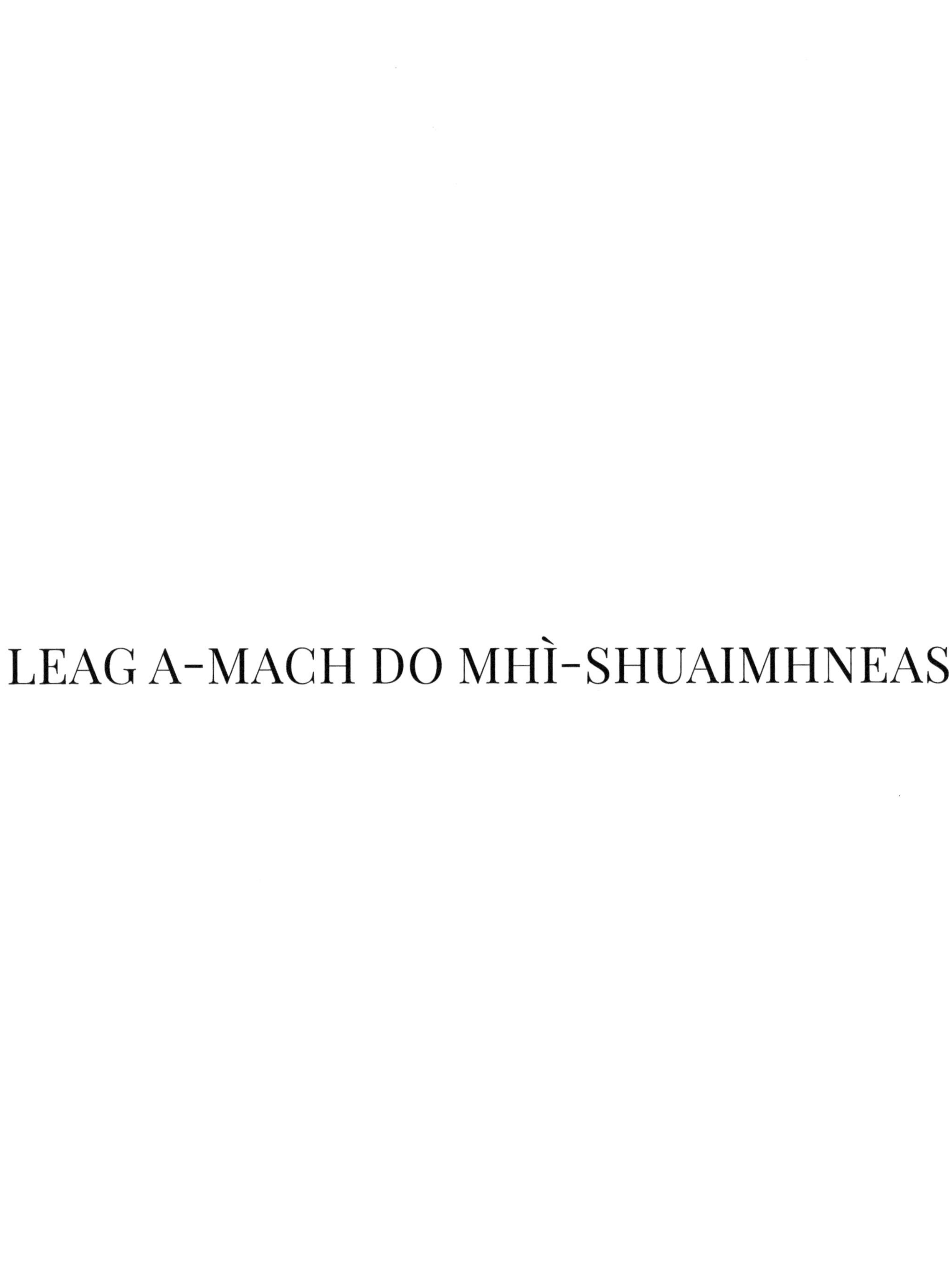

LEAG A-MACH DO MHÌ-SHUAIMHNEAS

www.ingramcontent.com/pod-product-compliance
Lightning Source LLC
LaVergne TN
LVHW070218110826
845147LV00003B/599

* 9 7 8 1 9 1 6 9 3 8 9 3 9 *